To my loving husband, Jim and my daughter, Brittany.

To my parents Earline & Horace Franklin,
whose love and support flow through me always.

To Oprah,
whose inspiration on the fateful trip led to this book being written.

Published by Afterwords Books

ISBN 13: 978-0-9854327-2-0
Library of Congress Control Number: 2014957365

First printing December 2014

Afterwords Books
P.O. Box 1534
New York, NY 10035-0821
info@awbooks.co
www.awbooks.co

Book design by Justin Lee Fulton
Author photo by Victor Powell

AfterWords
BOOKS

INTUITION

THE HIDDEN ASSET
EVERYONE SHOULD
LEARN TO USE

To:
Tanuja
In Love &
Light
Sheree Franklin

SHEREE FRANKLIN

CONTENTS

This book is meant to help you harness your God-given gift of intuition. Like most people, I was not endowed with special talents, skills or abilities in this area. My decision to learn how to trust my inner wisdom started when I became a full-time mom at home with my daughter. Without a doubt, I have made my share of mistakes in my life. To make better decisions in less time with less stress, I had to learn to hear my soul's voice.

Initially, I did not believe developing my inner wisdom would change my life. Instead, my desire was driven by a deep inner yearning to know more about myself. Like many of you, through the years, I have read a lot of New Age books, but nothing happened until a conscious shift occurred inside of me and I devoted myself to learning how to tap into my intuition.

Now we all know there are many skeptics who do not believe in intuition or even trust that it is a skill that can be harnessed by anyone other than psychics who have their signs displayed on oversized placards on the street. Trust me, I understand that. I am married to a CPA who does not believe anything that he does not see on a balance sheet.

What is unique about my approach — and this book — is that you will discover I am extremely open about explaining how developing my inner knowing impacted and changed different experiences in my life.

My hope is my book, *Intuition: The Hidden Asset Everyone Should Learn to Use*, will help you navigate your own life journey more effectively so that you do not hit the same potholes that I have run into.

Let's face it: Who really has time to learn how to use their intuition? Many of us are already far too busy. It is our inherent busyness, coupled with our being seduced by technology, which has led many of us to ignore our own valuable and powerful inner GPS.

Whether we know it or not, all of us are either consciously or unconsciously enrolled in what I call "Earth School." What I have come to realize is that if you live long enough and make enough mistakes, you will find your life is an invisible classroom that serves as a powerful teacher. This book will provide you with a spiritual boot camp of short and easy tools to help you test and examine your intuition at a deeper level.

The defining moment that led me to wanting to learn how to sharpen and strengthen my intuitive muscle began 28 years ago after the birth of my daughter, Brittany Marie Hogan. For me, her birth was like a magical doorway, helping me learn to develop the ability to listen to my soul's voice. And even though my marriage to her father did not last, I will always be eternally grateful for the freedom he gave me to stay home with our child, which allowed me to study the spiritual side of life. Before that time, I was too busy working to have time to explore my soul development.

Starting at the age of 12, I was already on my first job as a cashier in my family's grocery store. After graduating from high school, I achieved my goal of earning my bachelor's degree in journalism. And during my senior year in college, I was already employed as a broadcast reporter for a small television station. Following my reporting stint, I explored a variety of fields with jobs in public relations, marketing and insurance underwriting.

The best job in the world I have ever had is to be a mother. During the same time my daughter was learning the alphabet and numbers, I was a frequent visitor to the Chicago Public Library, where I read books on everything from meditation to intuition and spiritual development. Our living room doubled as a classroom for both of us, and sometime while watching Sesame Street with my child, I began to know myself at a deeper level.

As my confidence in being able to access my intuition grew, I began to believe it was possible for me to support myself without working a traditional job. But making the change from being a lifetime employee to business owner was not easy. The doorway for me opened during a chance meeting with a female entrepreneur I met at my health club. The woman owned a small advertising specialty distributorship and was an invaluable teacher on helping me to learn the industry. After working with her as an independent sales representative for a couple of years, I began to confront my fears about starting my own business.

Even allowing myself to think about going into business for myself was very scary because I lacked everything from a business plan to the finances to obtain a credit line. Instead of focusing on all the things I did not have, my first spiritual lesson was to concentrate on my strengths: the ability to access my intuition, and my very supportive family who did everything they could to help me succeed. The steps I took to create my life plan are the same ones I advise others to do when they want to achieve their dreams:

1. Expand your knowledge base by learning everything you can about the area of business you want to explore.

2. Have passion for whatever you want to do in your life and take every class or workshop you can to sharpen your tools.

3. Learn to trust and listen to your intuition.

During this period, I earned various small business certifications, and I became a graduate of both the Integrated Awareness and Avatar programs. (Integrated Awareness is a unique process developed by mentor and spiritual teacher Consuella C. Newton that links intuition and the conceptual mind for rapid control of awareness in just five days. The Avatar Program is a nine-day self-empowerment training delivered by a worldwide network of licensed Avatar Masters that guides others on discovering themselves so they will achieve their goals.) I also took classes on meditation and consciousness development along with healing courses focusing on Reiki and Soma Pi. (Reiki is a healing technique based on the principle that the therapist can channel energy into the patient by means of touch, to activate the natural healing processes of the patient's body and restore physical and emotional well-being. The Soma Pi technique was also developed by Newton. It is a preventative and healing health force that is used by certified practitioners all over the country.)

My search to discover myself is the same one many of you are facing who are reading this book. Many of us struggle with becoming the person we want to be. It takes longer than you thought and at times it may seem that you are moving in the right direction only to find you must start over again. Becoming your true self does not happen by accident. The fact is that if we are truly honest with ourselves, many of us are our own worst enemy. We are operating without the slightest clue about our intuition and how to let it guide us through periods of uncertainty.

Never has society needed this more than today, with so many people struggling to find meaning in their lives. Many of the challenges we face are a direct result of our own fears. This is what blocked me for a long time from being able to start my business.

At the time, I was going through a divorce, and I had no business plan or finances to start my new company. During this time, I also learned that maintaining a daily meditation practice was the only way for me to stay calm. Allowing myself to be quiet on a consistent basis gave me my first inkling of what it means to openly embrace your intuition as a valuable skill. There is no right or wrong way to connect with your inner compass. The challenge in embracing this skill is determined by your willingness to commit and the follow-through in taking action. Meditation is what worked for me.

After more than 20 years of studying and practicing using my intuition, I feel comfortable in sharing my knowledge. My ability to connect with my inner knowing was invaluable in growing my business and helping my transition in supporting others as an intuitive coach and counselor.

Listening to my inner knowing served me so well during my 17 years selling promotional products. My company, Specialties Plus, which started in 1989, was on a solid trajectory for success until 2005, when the Internet started to change things. Even though my company was having the best sales revenue in our history that year, I knew that things would not remain the same. During this time, once again I turned to my intuition to help me make the right decision. One day while in deep meditation, I heard a very distinct message from my inner wisdom. It said simply, "Your life as you know it now will not be the same in three months." Rather than reacting with trepidation or fear, I jumped up and threw my arms in the air and screamed out loud, "Change, that is great with me! I am ready for this!"

My reaction to circumstances changing in my life is an example of what Consuella C. Newton, author of *The Inner Quest*, explains. We have two choices when we are facing a major change: We must decide whether to be a volunteer or draftee. A volunteer is open and receptive to the growth. A draftee is dragged through, kicking and screaming.

We live on a planet of free will and have the ability to decide if we are "volunteers" when we are open and receptive to the growth. Operating at this level does not mean things will automatically work out. You will discover that your spiritual expansion will develop towards having a deep knowing that you will be guided in the right direction.

My willingness to be a volunteer led to me starting my company, which also played a pivotal role in me meeting and marrying the love of my life, James Hill, Jr. The two of us met when we were both business owners and members of the ROTARY/One Club in Chicago. To this day, I have jokingly said joining ROTARY/One was the best investment I ever made! Not only did I meet my future husband, I also networked with other corporate leaders, which led to a significant increase in my business. Hill is the retired founding senior partner of his own accounting firm, Hill Taylor LLC. (In 2009, his firm, one of the largest African-American owned accounting firms in the state of Illinois, merged with Mitchell & Titus, becoming the largest African-American owned accounting firm in the United States.) The support and love my husband has given me played a big part in me being able to embrace my destiny of becoming an intuitive coach and counselor.

It is not always easy for my CPA husband to understand what I do. The reality is I never planned to do any of this. Simply put, the work found me.

The opportunity for me to pursue my dream to turn my intuitive skill into a business model developed as the result of a chance encounter at a networking event with Melody Spann-Cooper, president of WVON-AM, a talk radio station in Chicago. She invited me to her station to be interviewed as a guest on a morning show to discuss opportunities for women to start their own businesses. My 30-minute interview expanded to an hour after a female listener called in to vent her frustrations over the challenges she faced in becoming an entrepreneur. The listener told me on that fateful day that the only way she could get a business started was if she got a miracle. Without any advance planning, I gave the caller my insight on how all of us have the power to manifest miracles in our lives. Suddenly, the radio station's phone lines lit up, and I continued to talk to other women and men who wanted to hear my comments on change and using intuition as a guide. The next day, Melody called and invited me back to WVON to produce a small, weekly segment discussing the importance of using your intuition. My stint on the radio station lasted about six months, long enough to develop a solid client base. This experience gave me the confidence to embrace my gift and begin seeing clients on my own.

The coincidence of events that led to Melody inviting me to be a guest on WVON-AM can best be described as a synchronicity. This occurs when a particular point in time serves to connect two or three incidents together, which unknowingly expands to a bigger picture and leads to a dramatic change in a person's life. I am forever grateful to Melody Spann-Cooper for the confidence and trust she placed in me.

With the knowledge that I have gained from my experiences, I want to help you too. In the following pages, you will find tips to:

1. Awaken your consciousness to recognize how intuition feels and reacts in your body.

2. Recognize synchronicities.

3. Develop a moral code for how you will conduct your life using your intuition.

4. Shape your relationships with forgiveness and reconciliation to eliminate the negative emotions of anger, shame, fear and resentment.

PART I

DISCOVER YOUR INTUITION

"You must train your intuition - you must trust the small voice inside you which tells you exactly what to say, what to decide." —*Ingrid Bergman*

Intuition is the hidden asset many of us take for granted. It is hard to define because it is based on a mixture of our inner awareness and our ability to process information in a way that benefits us. One of the most common ways we notice our intuition is when we are driving. Have you ever waited at a red light, and, right after the traffic signal changes, something tells you to keep your foot on the brake? And after following our hunch, we watch in amazement when another motorist runs the light and drives into the very space where our vehicle would have been, resulting in a serious accident if we had not obeyed our inner wisdom! It is as simple as that. Everyone has this innate ability, and we are using it every day, even when we are not conscious of it. When we learn to trust this skill, it is easy to discover how it benefits our lives.

The word intuition comes from Latin verb *intueri*, which means to look inside or to contemplate. This is my definition of our hidden asset:

Intuition is the God-given gift that gives each human the ability to sense and feel inside what is going on in and around us at all times. Our hidden asset is the invisible consciousness that protects, supports and helps to heal us in all areas of our lives. When we dedicate time to quieting our minds, this opens the doorway to connecting with our inner wisdom. The lessons we learn by strengthening our gift are non-ending, including helping us to know our life purpose and to grow into a strong spiritual consciousness.

Now that we have defined intuition, here are some of the terms you will find in this book that are used to describe it:

Gut reaction
Inner GPS
Inner wisdom
Higher consciousness
Hunch
Second sight
Premonition
Instinct
Clairvoyance

So, why do people take for granted their hidden asset? Many of us already recognize our ability, but we do not identify it as a tangible skill to help guide and direct our lives. **Here are the reasons why many people have difficulty connecting with their inner wisdom:**

1. Our minds are too cluttered with information.

2. Society views fact–based thinking as more valuable.

3. Technology has become our focal point to turn to for everything we need.

4. We ignore our emotions.

5. We have forgotten how to love ourselves.

In this Internet and social media world, we are bombarded with information in the way of blogs, videos and news alerts as well as countless advertisements. When you add in our work and family responsibilities, our super-active minds make it easy to ignore what is going on inside of us.

One of the best ways to quiet our mind is to develop a prayer and meditation practice. These are the two spiritual tools that open the doorway to our intuition. Meditation involves disconnecting from everything going on in and around us and choosing to be quiet. To do this effectively, we must turn off the mental chatter, analyzing, obsessing and worrying, and enter into a state of peace. You do not need a fancy place to begin this practice; what matters most in helping you to strengthen your intuitive muscle happens by consistently making the time to quiet our minds. Scientists tell us people who meditate for as little as 10 minutes a day can achieve health benefits like lowered blood pressure, decreased physical pain and a strengthened immune system. The way to ignite our meditation practice is by adding prayer; this creates the divine spark that is available to anyone who wants to expand their consciousness.

Prayer is the open communication with our Higher Power that allows us to address every concern, problem or question that we have inside. In other words, a consistent prayer and meditation practice helps us to develop a plan, a vision for what we want to create in our lives.

Let's face it: Our society is much more comfortable with pointing to hard facts to help us determine what to do. We have become conditioned to using logic, reasoning and fact-based thinking as the basis for our decisions and choices. But rather than devaluing our intuition, we should view it as a powerful ally to traditional forms of thinking, giving us an added bonus in handling every challenge we are facing.

It has become easier for us to push our intuition aside due to our ever-increasing dependence on technology. Today, many people keep their electronic devices on 24/7, making it obsolete for us to do our own creative thinking or even remember how to come up with an original idea. We turn to Google for many of the answers we need instead of even considering looking inward to tap into our intuition. Because we are more focused on technology and our material things, we are less aware and mindful of what is going on in and around us.

We are interacting with each other less and less today, due to most of our business and personal communications occurring via email, text messages and social media. Our dependence on technology robs us of the subtle awareness that occurs when we look a person directly in their eyes, hear their voice and notice their body language. In other words, we are no longer paying attention to the vital clues that give our intuition the information to help us in our human experience. Ultimately, this results in us ignoring our own thoughts, feelings and emotions.

Since our inner wisdom flows through our emotions, we need to pay attention to our feelings to help us guide and direct our lives. When we become aware of our emotional patterns, it is easy to start recognizing the ones we want to avoid — resentment, anger, jealousy, guilt and fear. One of the foremost researchers on emotions, Dr. Joe Dispenza, the author of *You Are the Placebo: Making Your Mind Matter*, has this to say about recognizing how we feel:

> *"...our awareness alone can have an important physical effect on our bodies and our health."*

Our ability to learn how to use our intuition is largely based on how we process our feelings. Many of us have a lot of stress in our lives directly related to things we are afraid of. Our dependence and obsession with technology plays a big role in how much fear we experience on a daily basis. It is not unusual for many people to sleep with their cell phone or tablet, check their messages throughout the night and be bombarded with constant alerts of news flashes on natural disasters, deadly accidents, war, celebrity deaths and violence in our own communities. (I do not advise people to sleep with their electronic devices.)

Contrary to popular belief, our fears are not all bad. This powerful emotion provides us with our greatest lessons for growth as we study our physical reactions and begin to instinctively know what triggers us. The feeling of fear, like all our other emotions, unfolds in our body and mind. Our brains register a reaction to danger in our fear center, the amygdala, which gives the signal to our body to react within a few milliseconds. (The amygdala is the almond-shaped matter inside our brain that regulates our emotions. It is very important in our emotional learning.) Fear blocks our intuition because it interrupts the process in our brain that allows us to notice non-verbal cues and other signs that help us determine what to do when we perceive danger.

The best way to counteract the effects of negative emotions is by developing the habit of making lifelong observations of our feelings. When we operate in this way, we are capable of controlling the stress in our lives via the thoughts, feelings and emotions we concentrate on each day.

This is why one of the first homework assignments I give to my clients is to set aside 30 minutes to think one time a day for two weeks. If you are like most of the people I talk to, this probably seems like an outrageous request, but if you value yourself highly, you will realize this small commitment will make a big difference in your life. The way I suggest my clients approach their "thinking time" is to consistently develop the habit of exploring the ideas in their minds of what they want to create in their life. By doing this assignment, this helps us to recognize how we talk to ourselves. It is only when we become aware of our inner dialogue that we embrace the power we all have to change our external circumstances. One of the big payoffs of completing this assignment is it will help you to become laser focused on your goals, dreams and desires. Keep a notebook of your observations and set the intention for your intuition to guide and direct you on your chosen path. When we make the time to focus on our life plan, this helps us to recognize the necessary changes that must be done to turn our dreams into reality. By tuning into our inner dialogue, we become aware that many of us have forgotten how to truly love ourselves. Loving the good and not-so-good aspects of ourselves is the bridge that connects us to our higher consciousness.

Unfortunately, it is easier for us to develop the habit of focusing on all the things that make us unhappy. We need to put into our minds positive feelings such as love, joy and peace on a daily basis. It may take practice to make this happen, but over time, by loving ourselves, we will hear our intuition with greater clarity.

One of the simplest ways to practice self-love is by verbally and silently saying, "I love you" when we are showering or putting on lotion each day. You can even do it while you're brushing your teeth. Our body needs to hear these three little words, and it does not matter who says it.

When we layer our body, mind and spirit with love before we go out in the world, it becomes easier for us to observe when a shift in our emotions occurs for any reason. We need to think of our body as our private laboratory that alerts us to our own internal warning signs of each of our emotions.

In my work, I have discovered there are three types of people who explore their intuition:

1. Seekers - individuals who are open to exploring all levels of life physically, mentally, emotionally and spiritually. Their

desire may be fueled by a recent event that has led them to examine their priorities, goals and values.

2. Wounded - people who are carrying emotional pain that prevents them from living the highest version of their life. Those who are open to healing, forgiving and releasing their old hurts are often the most posed for growth because they have set a firm intention for their life to be better.

3. Accelerators – individuals who have already taken steps to explore their soul and are seeking greater insight and wisdom to accelerate their life journey.

These are the benefits of connecting with your intuition:

- Developing the power to consciously shift out of negative emotions when necessary.
- Alerting us when something is right or wrong for us.
- Empowering us to make wise decisions in less time with less stress.
- Achieving our goals.
- Releasing worry and stress from our environment.
- Getting to know our soul direction and life purpose.
- Enlightening us when it is time to walk away from those who create emotional stress in our lives.
- Encouraging our efforts to lead a purpose-driven life.
- Expanding our faith.

One of the most powerful experiences of my life was when I was selected out of 100,000 people to be in the audience for Oprah's Ultimate Fan Show on September 10, 2010. Being chosen was like winning the trifecta. Not only did I get to be in the audience with that amazing energy that day, but I also found, as did the other 300 audience members, that Oprah was taking us all to Australia. The eight-day, seven-night trip gave me an unforgettable experience. Going on that journey allowed me to fulfill one of my lifetime dreams—to meet the Aboriginal people.

Being selected for the show reinforced what I have known all along—that an invisible thread connected me to Oprah 20 years before we ever met Down Under.

The first time I became aware of my connection to Oprah started in 1989, when I was trying to decide what career path to take after being a stay-at-home mom for close to four years with my daughter, Brittany. For months, I had been waging an internal battle, struggling about whether to take a job or to start my own business. At the time, I was in my first marriage and was selling on a part-time basis with a small promotional products firm. With no business plan or money, I stood a better chance of winning the lottery than becoming an entrepreneur. Finally, one night, a dream involving Oprah served as an omen for the path I should take.

In my vision, Oprah was talking to me about her soon-to-be published autobiography. Somehow, the entertainment mogul had come across something I had written and she wanted to include it in her book. After intense negotiations, Oprah offered to compensate me three cents for every book sold. Most people know to this day Miss O has not published such a book, but imagine if she did; the three cents per book would quickly amass into a sizeable amount of money.

Awakening from my dream, I sensed there was a deep inner message being revealed to me. Writing down all the details of my dream on an envelope on my nightstand, I carried it with me for days and read it over and over trying to decipher the true meaning. I believed the message revealed that starting my own business would begin with pennies and it would grow.

My decision to become an entrepreneur was critically important because, less than a year later, my marriage ended and I became the primary supporter for my daughter. As a single mother, my top concern was to make sure Brittany knew she was loved and that she got the best education possible to ensure her future. Being self-employed gave me the parenting freedom to be able to attend my daughter's school trips and assemblies while earning the income needed to support us both. Things did work out well for my only child; she has earned bachelor's and master's degrees.

Taking this leap was not easy. I was afraid all the time. There were so many sleepless nights where I tossed and turned, questioning whether I made the right decision to strike out on my own. Worrying about everything became a habit for me, from how to pay all the bills to being a good mother.

Becoming a business owner allowed me to connect with the same entrepreneurial roots I developed as a teenager working in my father's grocery store on Chicago's south side. After my decision to follow the omen from my dream involving Oprah, it was not unusual for me to have very detailed dreams recalling the years my family worked together in my dad's store. I welcomed those dreams like an old friend, and they helped me to connect with the same feelings of pride and strength my family felt as we built my dad's business. Allowing those memories to resurface was the final confirmation that my intuition was letting me know my decision to work for myself was the right one.

Even though I felt intuitively guided to start my own company, there were many nights that I could not sleep for worrying, and I would often drag myself out of bed in the wee hours of the morning to watch The Oprah Winfrey Show reruns. Sitting on my couch in my pajamas, I often felt that Oprah's comments were being directed to me personally, even though the show was for millions of viewers. The wisdom she gave me during this critical period in my life never ceases to amaze me.

I never talked about that fateful dream which happened over 25 years ago until being interviewed as part of the application process to be on Oprah's Ultimate Fan Show. During a telephone interview with one of the show's producers, something eerie happened. When I recalled the details of the dream, the producer suddenly became very quiet and asked me to hold on. She returned to the call and introduced a second producer, who was now also on the line, and requested that I go through my entire interview process again.

As the talk with the two producers drew to a close, I was asked the final question posed to all of the Ultimate Fan applicants: "What is your dream?" I told them that my dream had always been to meet the Aboriginal people, having fallen in love with their story after reading the novel *Mutant Message Down Under* by Marlo Morgan many years before.

The two producers ended the telephone call with me by reading from what sounded like a prepared script: "There is no guarantee with this phone call you will be selected for Oprah's Ultimate Fan Show. That decision will be made at a later date and time."

My husband, Jim, listened to the entire interview with me. As soon as the call ended, I jumped up from my seat and asked him, "Do you want to go with me to The Oprah Winfrey Show?"

"Perhaps you did not hear what they said," he replied. "You are not going to be selected. Don't blow this out of proportion."

Believing that my presence on the show was divinely directed, I quickly replied, "I have visualized myself with a seat in the audience. The only question is, do you want to come with me?"

When he said "No," I picked up my cellphone and invited my childhood friend Gail Baker to go with me even before I had been officially notified I would be in the audience.

Taking Gail with me was very important because the person who attended the show automatically became your traveling companion to Australia.

As you can imagine, there were a couple of tense days around my house when my husband Jim first realized that his decision not to join me on Oprah meant he would not go with me on the world class trip Down Under.

From the moment I found out about the trip, each morning I woke up excited. This reminded me of how it felt to be a small child too excited to fall asleep on Christmas Eve. From September to December, I buzzed with a wonderful energy that often made me feel like dancing around my apartment. Two weeks before we were scheduled to leave, I learned that Oprah handpicked me to be included in a special group of twelve women who would travel on a once-in-a-lifetime trip to an Aboriginal ancient site in the Northern Territory. I will never forget being in the grocery store when the fateful call came in from one of the show's producers. I jumped for joy right in front of the cashier.

Sensing the deep mystical connection of this experience, I prepared for the trip by meditating and sending light and love to the Aboriginal people for the next two weeks. In addition, I dedicated time each morning to focus my intentions on what I wanted to create during my visit. There were three things I wanted to manifest:

1. I will share an intimate experience with Oprah.

2. I will create infinite opportunities and wonderful adventures in Australia with people who will become my lifelong friends.

3. I am opening the spiritual doorway to the Aboriginal people by sending them love and light.

To seal in the power of my intentions, I focused on this list and practiced a form of psychological acupressure called the Emotional Freedom Technique, or EFT. It is based on tapping on the same meridians that are used in traditional acupuncture to treat physical and emotional aliments. Finally, the day came for Gail and me to make the life-changing trip to Australia.

We flew from Chicago to Los Angeles and stayed overnight to meet the other 300 Ultimate Fans who would be flying on two planes to Australia. It was a grueling 15 hours from Los Angeles to Sydney, Australia. Once we arrived, people went to their assigned groups based on our destinations, which were identified by animal totem names. The group I was designated to be in was named the Frilled Neck Lizards and consisted of 12 amazing women with whom I traveled to see the Aborigines. I am honored to call them my friends today.

The Frilled Neck Lizards was the only group of Oprah's 300 Ultimate Fans outfitted with custom-sized cowboy hats, western-style shirts and raincoats. All of the groups started on their assigned journeys the very next day after arriving in Sydney.

My group's trip to the Northern Territory began with a Qantas flight, continued on a private plane and finally ended with a helicopter ride. My eyes reeled from the shock of everything we saw as we made this journey. We looked down on fertile lush land with rolls of grass and waterfalls. It was my very first helicopter ride, and at times I wanted to pinch myself as proof that this was really happening.

We were treated to a historic visit to Gabarnmung Cave, a rock shelter owned by the Jawoyn tribe of Australia's Northern Territory. The site is covered with Aboriginal paintings dating back 35,500 years[1]. Before our arrival, only 26 non-indigenous visitors had ever been invited into this sacred space, a naturally formed temple nestled in a sandstone foundation covered by hundreds of ancient Aboriginal rock paintings.

The site was rediscovered on a routine helicopter run in 2006 by the Jawoyn Association's cultural and environmental manager Ray Whear and pilot Chris Morgan. (Jawoyn is an all-encompassing expression used in reference to language, culture, people and territory of the Aboriginal people who are traditionally connected to south-west Arnhem Land. This area has one of the highest concentrated areas of rock art sites in the world—it's world famous for its rock paintings located in the ancient and hidden site of Gabarnmung Cave.)

The memory of our group taking off in three large helicopters is seared in my mind, and sometimes, even now, that sight appears in my dreams.

When we arrived, the temperature was a stifling 105 degrees. We walked a short distance to meet the Jawoyn elders who greeted the women in our group with a special blessing, which included rubbing a mixture of oil and herbs directly on our heads. The elders confided that preparation for our arrival included them contacting their Aboriginal ancestors to get their approval for our visit, and that weather changes would be occurring to signify their agreement for us to be on the sacred land.

Traveling with our group of 12 women to Gabarnmung Cave were Oprah's film crew and producers, a film documentary crew and executives from the Australian Tourism Bureau. As soon as the group of more than 30 people was safely under the covering of the rock shelter, the skies opened up with a hard downpour. This was the first

1. The Jawoyn Association, Gabarnmung: an Ancient and Hidden Site

weather change to occur after arriving at the cave and it signified the ancestors' approval of our visit.

Arriving on the sacred site for me was like crossing the invisible line between the past and the present. The downpour faded into the background as all of us became mesmerized listening to the oral history and detailed stories of Aboriginal life. The elders spoke of the past with so much feeling and detail that it sounded like they could have easily been reading from a history book. We learned later that the details told to us were etched deeply in their memories since, they explained, none of them could read or write. It is a part of the Aboriginal tribe's commitment to know their history and to embrace it with their heart and soul. Explaining their tribe's connection with the past, Jawoyn elder Margaret Katherine told us, "People who live without their culture live in slavery."

One of the most disturbing aspects of this trip was when the Jawoyn elders shared with our group their painful stories of siblings that were forever lost to them. These relatives were forcibly taken from their families as a result of removal policies put into place by Australian federal, state and territory governmental agencies and church missions from the 1880s to the 1970s. The removal policy placed upon Aboriginal children with European ancestry was commonplace, when one parent was "white" and the other Aboriginal. The objective of the removal was racial assimilation, which resulted in the loss of indigenous culture, language and identity.

The Aboriginals are the true natives of Australia. How they endured the violence of European settlers who took their land and forced family members apart both deeply saddens and shocks me. Their suffering is part of the legacy of the Aboriginal people that is still reflected in the Australian way of life, due to their poor living conditions and lack of opportunities.

Listening firsthand to the extreme hardships they faced is different than reading it in a book. My eyes filled with tears and I knew intuitively why the sky opened up with rain when we entered Gabarnmung Cave. The downpour to me symbolized the heartfelt pain that the Aboriginal people have lived with for over 200 years and what they are still facing in being ostracized in Australia.

Once the downpour ended, our group exited the rock shelter and we were shocked to discover the sweltering 105 degrees we first arrived in had now dropped to a cool 75 degrees. This was the second weather change validated by the Aboriginal ancestors. We were treated to a feast of Aboriginal vegetables, fruits and fish. The two long tables covered by white linen tablecloths and all the fixings had been flown in with painstaking detail by helicopter in preparation for our trip. We barely had time to enjoy this feast when our pilots announced we had to leave the sacred site before dark. Our time with the Jawoyn elders quickly drew to an end.

Before leaving, our group lined up in front of Margaret Katherine and the other elders to say our goodbyes. Standing in front of her, with our hands entwined, I felt tingly inside when the dark brown-skinned woman said to me, "Sheree, your spirit has already touched mine." The words she spoke to me felt surreal, especially because I had no memory of ever being introduced to Margaret Katherine. After we left the ancient site, I wondered if the words I heard really took place or if they were part of a dream I had after traveling to the ancient site. It was only during a chance encounter with one of Oprah's producers that Katherine's statement to me was confirmed. The female producer and I spoke briefly when all the Ultimate Fans were reunited at a fantastic party at the Sydney Harbour. To this day, I regret not remembering the producer's name, but I will never forget what she told me. By now, Oprah's producers and staff had carefully vetted all of the Ultimate Fans and it surprised me when the woman called me by my name and asked, "Are you Sheree?" When I confirmed that I was, she said, "It was something hearing what Margaret Katherine said to you." Needless to say, I was astounded to hear her confirmation of words I was not sure had been uttered. I replied with complete shock: "I did not know if that was real or part of a dream." The female producer told me that Katherine's words to me had even been captured on videotape. My eyes filled with tears.

All of the Frilled Neck Lizards felt deeply emotional about the time we spent with these ancient people. During the time we said our goodbyes to the Aboriginal elders, many of the other women in my group were openly crying. As our helicopters lifted off, a sudden wind shift occurred which caused our large choppers to sway from side to side. The two pilots steering my helicopter looked equally surprised when the sudden wind gust started, and they studied their instrumentation and charts on their laptops, trying to determine what was happening. As quickly as the wind picked up, it suddenly stopped, and we were treated to the spectacular sight of a sky of pink framed by double rainbows forming as we lifted off. This was the third and final weather change that signified the ancestors' approval of our being on the sacred site. This final testament of the ancestors' authority that is still present in the ancient land treated us to a cosmic masterpiece as our helicopters lifted off.

One Frilled Neck Lizard, Mary Hodder, gave this description of the time spent in the ancient site:

> *"Standing in the cave with all of you and Margaret Katherine, life really began for me. I laid down years of pain in that cave. Long years of sorrow and defeat and not believing I could ever be happy. As we lifted off in the helicopters, I knew that my life direction was going to be different from then on. I got this 'woman power thing' inside me that I have held*

onto ever since. I chose a different way of being in the world. And I am not trying to say that it has been easy ever since. No, the struggles come and go. There is still pain. But nothing can stop me or dissuade me from what I most desire."

I often wonder how my life would have turned out if I had set an intention to have my own television show on the OWN network. My "show" would feature the stories of people who used their intuition and synchronistic moments to change their lives. This taught me what I have known all along—that we are all much more powerful than we realize and we should all dream bigger dreams.

Since the trip, my group has met for an annual reunion twice, traveling from as far away as Canada, Washington, California and Tennessee to spend time with each other. Lifelong friends now, when we are together, we always reflect and talk about our experiences in the ancient land.

Returning from Australia, I knew the one thing that still needed to be done was for me to write my first book. This is my way of honoring the final bit of advice Oprah shared with us when we were at the airport waiting to return home: "Don't let going to Australia be the biggest thing you do in your life. You must go back and achieve new dreams and goals."

As Miss O was saying goodbye to the loud group of her Ultimate Fans, right before we were to board our plane, our eyes met and I touched my heart, symbolizing my love for her and that moment, and I ended our connection by blowing her a kiss. She repeated the same gesture back, confirming for me once again the invisible connection that continues to exist between us.

The friends I met on that life-altering trip to the ancient land also played an instrumental role in the writing of this book. Originally, I was planning to write about minority women and change. Despite having done a number of interviews for the book, I struggled with writing it. It was during our second Frilled Neck Lizards reunion that the women reminded me of the sage advice from Margaret Katherine: "Before you can tell someone else's story you must first tell your own."

Hearing those words had a big impact on me. I felt intuitively drawn to stop writing my original book and to write the one you are now reading.

Here are the 10 lessons that I learned in Australia. They are valuable tools for anyone who wants to learn how to use their intuition:

1. Always have a dream.
2. Believe that anything can happen.
3. Be excited every day about your life.
4. Do not wait to be seated in a helicopter before you see things from a higher perspective.
5. Always make time to connect with your spirit.
6. Consistently set goals and follow through to turn your dreams into reality.
7. Always dream bigger dreams.
8. Laugh often.
9. Welcome new friends into your life.
10. Recognize moments of synchronicity and take action.

In September 2014, Prime Minister Tony Abbott took the unprecedented step of spending time in a remote Australian eucalyptus forest to gain firsthand knowledge of the painful injustice experienced by the Aborigines for many decades. He believes that the British settlers were responsible for the atrocities endured by the Aboriginal people. "Mr. Abbott proposes rewriting the constitution, formally to recognize Aborigines as the nation's first peoples – a change which he argues, would help to complete the national journey towards reconciliation, 226 years after the first settlers arrived.[2] " My hope is that Prime Minister Abbott's visit lights a fire in Australia and brings hope and promise to the lives of the Aborigines.

2. Pearlman, Jonathan. "Out in the Bush, Abbott Attacks Britain's Aboriginal Sins." Telegraph 22 September 2014.

Long before I traveled to Australia, my intuition guided me to plan a meditation to give during our trip. My intention for doing this was to make a contribution for being invited on this once-in-a-lifetime experience. You will notice my "gift" did not require a financial investment. This is often what blocks many of us from "earning our seat" because we are afraid to believe that our talents, skills and abilities are enough. As a result, we allow our own fears and insecurities to prevent us from shining with the light of our soul.

Until now, I have never shared the intimate details leading up to my creating the moment of reflection for everyone to feel connected right before we were to leave for the ancient site. My process started immediately after being informed by Oprah's staff that I would be included in the small group that would travel to the Northern Territory. The very next day after hearing the news, I woke up like everyone else does, trying to shake the cobwebs out of my head, when suddenly something different happened. Without any effort on my part, my mind came up with a vision of me doing a meditation in Australia. And as it continued to happen each morning, I decided to engage my imagination playfully and just enjoy the inner playground that was going on inside of me. What was happening to me I believe can best be described as a serendipitous vision. At first, watching the images float through my mind was like having my own private feel-good movie. It was only after a day or two that it dawned on me to take notes and begin to prepare the actual meditation practice that would be shared. There's no doubt in my mind that the intuitive hunch to tap into my imagination was part of the cosmic chess game that everyone was unconsciously playing who had the good fortune to be on the trip to Gabarnmung Cave.

In hindsight, it was totally irrational for me to expect that my "intuitive hunch" to lead a meditation would fit into the hectic, fast-paced back-to-back agenda planned for us. We discovered the full extent of the elaborate planning for the Frilled Neck Lizards in a meeting only a couple of short hours after we arrived at the InterContinental Hotel in Sydney, Australia.

When I entered the meeting room with my friend, Gail, we felt the same electrifying feeling we first experienced at Oprah's show months earlier. There is no doubt in my mind that all the Frilled Neck Lizards sensed the same thing, as everyone's eyes were stretched wide as if they were wondering what would happen next. Within minutes of our sitting down, the details of our travel plans to go to the Northern Territory were delivered with enthusiasm by the top executives of Tourism Australia, Tourism Northern Territory and Event Architects, Chicago.

The Northern Territory of Australia covers a massive portion of the country. This area occupies about one sixth of Australia's total land mass and covers 520,902 square miles. If you compared this region to the state of Texas, it would be double the size. The area is best known as being the site of the country's most sacred treasures: the Aboriginal people and their culture. The tourism executives shared with our group that we would be visiting an ancient site so remote that few people ever go there. They told us, "Everyone will covet your trip."

We all received a package that held a nine-page color document devoted exclusively to our private trip. This was our first glimpse into the carefully detailed plans that went into the precisely-timed schedule for our three days in the Northern Territory. We also found out that organizing our trip was so involved that the plans were only finalized two days before we landed in Sydney. As soon as I received my package, my mind zeroed in on our trip to Gabarnmung Cave, which was scheduled for the very next day. Each of the 12 women in my group listened with rapt attention while peppering the tourism executives with as many questions as possible to find out all the details we could. Afterwards, we were quickly ushered to the back of the room where tailors and fitters were waiting to outfit us with custom outback hats, shirts and raincoats. The tailoring service operated at such an accelerated pace that all of our group's alterations, which included embroidering "Oprah's Ultimate Australian Adventure" logos on our shirts and raincoats, were done that same night, and our clothes were delivered in bright red garment bags that were put inside our hotel rooms when we returned from dinner.

As you can imagine, there was no time for me to find out if my group would be receptive to doing the meditation I had planned. We barely went to sleep that night and had to get up at 6 a.m. the next day to board the first of three flights.

Leading our group on this historic trip was the wonderful team of professionals from Event Architects (now known as agencyEA), Chicago who we affectionately nicknamed "Blue Shirts." They were our "handlers" who had the task of making sure our talkative, laughing group stayed on our strict schedule. The very tough and highly professional producer extraordinaire, David St. Martin, kept us in a constant state of motion to ensure that our packed schedule ran like clockwork. To top it off, our activities, like all the other Oprah Ultimate Fans, operated under a tight veil of secrecy, and we were told not to reveal our plans to the Australian news media that followed us whenever they could. Things were moving at such a hectic pace that I bet the others, like me, barely had time to process the significance of our trip to Gabarnmung.

It was during the second leg of our trip when we were on the private plane that I decided to approach St. Martin with my request. You should have seen the look he gave me when I asked if I could do a short meditation for the Frilled Neck Lizards. Not realizing the full extent of the trip's details, I mistakenly thought my meditation could be easily done in a small space with only our group present. Imagine my surprise when right before we were to board our helicopters, one of Oprah's producers called me to the front of the room and announced I would be given exactly 10 minutes to do my meditation in the small pre-boarding space we were all gathered in.

There were 30 people crammed into the small airport hangar as we waited to board the three large copters outside. Included in the room were the 12 women in the Frilled Neck Lizards, Oprah's staff (consisting of both cameramen and producers), documentary filmmakers, rock art specialist Ben Gunn, and members of the Australia tourism bureaus including Malarndirri McCarthy, the Northern Territory minister of tourism at that time.

This is what earning your seat is all about. You cannot plan or predict the exact details for offering your "gift," and once you set the intention to give, you must be ready at a moment's notice. Two things helped to prepare me for this moment: my passion for helping others to meditate and the countless number of speeches I had given while being a member of Toastmasters International. This is what earning your seat requires; each of us must develop the ability to determine our own destiny by constantly developing new skills. And you must be open to the unexpected twists and turns that happen once your plan is put into motion.

Walking to the front of the room, I may have appeared outwardly calm, but believe me, with each step I took, my heart was pounding in my chest. Rising up from my seat when my name was called, the first thing I did was to remind myself to stand straight. Our posture communicates non-verbal messages about us all the time, and even if you are inwardly nervous, displaying a strong body and a warm smile will do wonders to help you appear confident. Right before I got ready to speak, my intuition reminded me in the soft voice that I have come to recognize as a trusted friend, "This is your gift to give today." Despite hearing this reassurance from my inner wisdom, I was still trying to will myself to be outwardly calm as the entire roomful of people gave me their attention. To help me focus, I used a technique known as "sated strength." Mastering this ability requires that no matter what is going on, you appear to be perfectly satisfied and at ease with your surroundings. In their book, *Compelling People: The Hidden Qualities that Make Us Influential*, co-authors John Neffinger and Matthew Kohut describe this technique as being an important reservoir to tap into whenever you feel overwhelmed.

Keep in mind that despite my having taught numerous meditation classes before, I was totally shocked by the sudden twist of going to the front of the room filled with people from all over the world, with Oprah's cameramen filming the whole thing. To earn your seat, you must be totally and completely comfortable with yourself and recognize the feeling of fear when it first comes up inside of you. Whenever I notice fear in my body, I treat this powerful emotion "like an old friend" and consciously decide what strategy I need to change things. In that moment, as I stood before everyone, my way of handling being afraid was to focus on the friendly faces of my Frilled Neck Lizards. Recently, I touched base with my group member, Michelle Fizzard, and the two of us discussed the impact my meditation had on her that day. This is what she shared with me:

> *"I remember being in the small airport hangar where you gave your meditation, and how the energy of the room filled my soul, and I felt more grounded in myself. (I needed that since everything was moving*

so quickly.) I believe those precious moments when you stood before us prepared our hearts and souls for an unforgettable spiritual experience, one each of us was meant to experience. I was changed that day."

Moments before I started my meditation, I sensed a unique energy present in the room. There is no way to explain it other than to tell you everything moved in slow motion inside of me. This is how it feels to operate in a state of pure consciousness; you become aware of only the present moment. Most of the time our thoughts bounce back and forth between the past and the future, and we fail to recognize the power of what it means to be truly aware in the present moment.

I flowed into the energy of the meditation, fully loving and embracing that my dream of spending time with the Aboriginal people was coming true. Have you ever had a feeling so strong that you had a strong "gut reaction," that you just knew it was the right thing to do? This is what happened to me in my plan to guide everyone that day to feel connected. I felt a little lightheaded as we all entered together into a space of oneness.

This is the first affirmation I recited in that crowded room just before our historic helicopter ride:

I Am the Light,
The Light is within me
The Light moves throughout me
The Light surrounds me
The Light protects me
I Am the Light. [3]

The entire room completed the meditation I planned for them, which consisted of two other energy-raising exercises. Afterwards, a feeling

---

3. © Consuella C. Newton, 1986

of complete peace filled the space to the point where I noticed the tear-filled eyes of the people who were standing in front of me. Even one of Oprah's cameramen pulled me aside that night at the hotel to tell me about the wonderful, loving feeling that flowed in the room during my meditation. One of my group members, Stacy Carter, summed it up best: "During the few moments of quiet, this helped me to remember and recognize how special we were to be in the place we were."

Going on that trip helped me to remember, once again, how powerful we are when we listen to our intuition and take action. When we become aware and follow our inner knowing, we are playing a role in creating the future we desire, and it is often the smallest actions we take that expands our lives in ways we never imagined. Was I afraid of doing the meditation in front of the roomful of distinguished strangers that day? Yes, of course I was. But we all live on a free-will planet, and we can choose to express our inner splendor and glory in simple ways every day. And while you may not have a world-class experience to spur you to take action, each of us can set our own intention to contribute to raising the consciousness of everyone we encounter by giving our gifts freely. When you operate at this level, it might involve giving a person your seat on the bus or train as you travel to work, holding the door for a stranger who is walking behind you, or allowing the energy of grace to flow through you when listening to a trusted friend repeat the same story she has told you several times while, of course, most importantly, maintaining a consistent habit of listening to and following your soul's voice.

The interconnectedness of my giving the meditation became crystal clear to me the same night after we visited the sacred cave, as I quickly fell into an exhausted sleep and dreamed of Jawoyn elder Margaret Katherine. During my dream, she told me, "Synchronicities will be occurring the next day that will reward you for your gift."

It was hard to imagine that after going on the once-in-a-lifetime adventure to visit the ancient site, things could get any better. But the next day, our group had an unbelievable surprise when Miss O herself arrived via helicopter to join us when we were scheduled to visit Uluru (Ayers Rock) – Kata Tjuta (The Olgas) National Park. The heat was a sizzling 105 degrees, and all of the Frilled Neck Lizards quickly circled around the media mogul, wearing our blue outback shirts and hats. The photo of us all together made the front page of many of the Australian newspapers and was picked up by national media across the U.S.

Anyone who saw the three shows on the Australian Adventure knows Oprah had a low tolerance for the December summer heat. She quickly took charge and urged us all to get back on the ultra-modern bus that took the Frilled Neck Lizards around. While she was on the bus with us, everyone in our group was a mishmash of nervous energy and we snuck pictures of her like children who were trying to hide the candy they had received at Halloween.

To our excitement, Oprah's visit spiraled into three more fabulous events that same day. First, she joined us for a sunset cocktail hour on the mountaintop; next, Miss O attended a private dance ceremony by the Aborigines; and the biggest moment by far was when the entertainment queen shared an intimate dinner with us. We were the only group out of all the Ultimate Fans with whom Oprah made the time to share an entire day.

The biggest part of this spellbinding, dazzling day happened for me later that same night at dinner when I was shocked to discover that my seat was right next to Oprah's. I was so shell-shocked over seeing my name on the place card that I pulled one of the show's producers aside to question whether the seating arrangement was correct. At that point, with all the excitement and elaborate travel plans we had been through over the last two action-packed days, I was struggling to keep my mind clear to try to remember everything that was going on around me. The words in my dream from Margaret Katherine radiated and resonated in my heart that night as I chatted with Oprah. She was warm and engaging and made everyone in the room feel like we were all one family.

Everyone has the same unlimited potential to manifest their own once-in-a-lifetime experience. We are all more powerful than we realize in creating our future when we express our gifts, talents and abilities without fear. After all, we are all just mirrored images of each other. The same thing that happened to me can very easily happen to you. I know you are thinking you will not have a world-class experience with Oprah, but you never know how the cosmic chess game in your life will play out. None of us do. To operate at this level, you must simply commit to being a selfless team member and reveal your gifts at the moment you feel intuitively drawn to act. To earn your seat, you must fully engage in loving every moment of your life and use your imagination to envision yourself living the future you want to create.

There is no doubt in my mind that had I not created my meditation "gift," Oprah probably would not have asked to be seated next to me at our surprise dinner.

To recap, here are the five steps to take to earn your own seat:

1. Use your imagination and fully engage all your senses to visualize the future you want to create.

2. Experience life unselfishly and be willing to give to others.

3. Recognize how fear feels in your body and determine the steps you need to take to shift out of it.

4. Trust that everything happens in the divine time and place.

5. Create an easygoing process to reach your true potential by continuing to take classes, sharing minds with people who

encourage you and being open to developing new talents, skills and abilities.

PART II
STAY OPEN TO EVERY OPPORTUNITY TO LEARN

Chance encounters offer ripe opportunities for wonderful "click" moments to occur, which allow us to have unexpected connections with the people that many times can lead to our greatest life's lessons. This happened to me one morning when I ran into "Susan," one of my neighbors, in the building elevator where we both live. This random moment served as a significant lesson on what it means to take action and manifest whatever you need.

Susan, 65, is a highly successful businesswoman who thrives on being on top of breaking financial news. Usually, whenever we see each other, she is rushing to get to the airport or attending one of the high-powered events in the Windy City.

This particular morning, I sensed something was different with her, and I knew, on a deep level, that Susan was sad. What came to mind as we exchanged pleasantries is that she felt "the party was over" and that she would never find a man to love her.

This savvy, business-minded executive who sits on various corporate boards has achieved tremendous professional success, but after being divorced three times and having her last relationship end, Susan was giving up on love.

Even though we lived in the same building for over 10 years, until that day, we had never had a personal conversation. It took me only a couple of seconds to formulate a plan to try to talk to Susan on a deeper level. I decided to turn the conversation to seeking her advice on what to wear to an upcoming formal event. To my surprise, Susan offered to look over my dress options and suggested that I come up to her apartment later in the day so she could check out my wardrobe choices.

Her invitation struck me as a moment of pure serendipity, since before this day we never had a real conversation with each other. As I exited the elevator, I counseled myself on taking things slowly when we talked again.

I decided when I saw Susan later to allow our moments together to flow naturally and brought up my dresses for her to see at our scheduled time.

Sitting across from Susan reaffirmed what I have always known: Emotional pain does not discriminate. You can be on top of the world and still find yourself nursing a broken heart. I knew that getting Susan to open up about what was really causing a heavy pain around her heart would have to occur at the right time and moment.

Very cautiously, I approached the subject of meditation as a valuable tool to provide inner guidance in difficult times. My words felt awkward as I walked the delicate line of trying not to invade her privacy while gently opening a doorway to a discussion that I knew needed to happen.

She did just what I expected and responded with her razor sharp wit, saying that she "had only recently committed to flossing her teeth and she didn't have time for anything else."

"Well, how is your soul doing?" I shot back softly.

Susan looked at me differently, and we began to discuss what it means to have a spiritual connection in life. Talking with her at length, I shared with her my sense that her soul wanted to make a romantic connection. My sense was that Susan being open to love was the only way to open the doorway to all of life's opportunities. After going through the relationship rollercoaster, Susan felt she would never get what she truly wanted most in her life.

To me what happened between us that day are the "click" moments that are the cornerstones for being able to strengthen your intuitive muscles.

As Susan and I sat side by side on her bed that day, we talked candidly about her past relationships that had not worked out. Despite her tremendous professional success, I saw a vulnerable side that had not been revealed before. Sharing at this level led my new friend to generously offer to loan me a bracelet to wear with my dress. This special connection between us was interrupted when the phone rang in her bedroom.

Susan was hesitant about answering the call since she told me that the line ringing was an old number that she had not given out to anyone in a very long time. The caller turned out to be someone from her distant past, a college boyfriend she had not spoken to in over 35 years.

Wanting to give them a chance to talk alone, I collected my dresses and the bracelet she loaned me, and gently nudged Susan and whispered, "There are no accidents."

The phone call proved to be an important one because after their talk, the two made plans to rekindle their friendship and Susan invited him to come for a visit that month. Despite the years of being out of touch, the two reconnected as if the time apart never happened. Susan and her college boyfriend have maintained an exclusive, committed relationship for the last 10 years. Now whenever I run into the highly-driven financial expert, she often shares this story of us talking in the elevator with her friends and business associates, telling them after our encounter she has come to believe that "there are no accidents."

Intuitive moments in our lives show up when we allow ourselves to be open and receptive to experiencing life fully when it happens. Opening herself up to love has changed Susan on a deeper level, resulting in her shifting her business focus to one of being of service. She credits this change as playing a powerful factor in being in high demand as a speaker. Her lectures are always packed, and she has a waiting list of people who scramble for a few minutes of her time.

Our talk that day also served as a wake-up call for me about uncovering a painful truth in my own life. After wearing the bracelet she loaned me to the black tie event, I left it out on my dresser, planning to return it to Susan. The next day my cleaning woman Karina, who worked with my family for five years, was in my apartment. After she left, I noticed the bracelet was missing and questioned her about where it could be. She claimed to have never seen the piece of jewelry, and this led me to doing a frantic search to find the item so it could be returned to Susan. To my surprise, many of the boxes I had in one drawer where I kept necklaces and bracelets were all empty. Without taking the time to talk in the elevator that day with Susan, I would not have known the person I trusted to clean my home was stealing me blind.

There is no way to prove that my cleaning lady stole my missing jewelry. A police report was filed and I immediately stopped using Karina's services. Since that incident, nothing has ever turned up missing in my home again. My desire to help Susan by sharing my intuitive insight with her led to me also being helped.

I believe that when our intuition surfaces, we release our tendency to be in a rush and ignore the subtle energy around us. The more spontaneous moments we allow ourselves to experience increase our chances of stumbling onto a new idea or even the opportunity to have something disclosed which had been hidden. This is the reason why embracing random powerful encounters is so important, because it often serves as an opening for an unexpected outcome.

Our brains have been designed to accept order rather than random encounters. Being open to new experiences is often just what we need to jolt us out of our comfort zone and propel us forward to achieving our hopes, dreams and desires.

When recalling this incident with Susan, she said it is clear to her that without my request to assist with my dress selection, she would never have been home on a weekday afternoon to receive the fortuitous phone call from her old college boyfriend. And she also notes that it was due to my gentle nudging that she paid attention and acted on her own intuition to invite her college boyfriend to visit her.

If we want to develop our intuitive muscle, we must be open to using it and trusting it when things present themselves in our lives. This is how the invisible becomes visible to us. Inner wisdom is a powerful language that we must use to guide, direct and inspire ourselves to live the highest version of our lives.

Here are the tips for helping you to pay attention to your intuition:

1. Realize that casual meetings can often turn out to be milestone moments in our lives.

2. Develop the habit of telling yourself "you always have enough time" rather than rushing and believing the opposite. Our busyness often blocks our ability to recognize critical clues that are right in front of us.

3. Pray to be divinely directed and guided in everything you do each day.

When a 63-year-old woman walked into my office, the first thing I noticed was a large bandage on her right hand. Glancing at her face, I knew intuitively she would rather be anywhere else than coming to see me for an appointment that day. What I have noticed in my work as an intuitive counselor and coach is paying attention to the small and large details helps me to sense what is going on even before I have spoken to a new client. Her expression was so unpleasant that she looked like someone who had eaten something sour. Our session started right there with me sharing my insight before she even told me what was going on with her hand.

In my work, I have learned to accept that most people need time to warm up before feeling comfortable enough to freely discuss what they hope to gain from an appointment with me. I offered "Tara," a divorce attorney, a cup of tea hoping that this would make her feel more relaxed. As we sat across from one another sipping tea, I found out the bandage on the middle finger of her right hand was due to a very serious health condition.

Three months earlier, a wound developed on her finger that would not heal. She scheduled a doctor's appointment, expecting to get a quick prescription that would clear it up. However, after her doctor carefully examined the open sore, additional tests were immediately ordered, which determined the origin of the infection to be a flesh-eating bacteria. This is a rare infection of the deeper layers of the skin and tissues. Typically, this type of infection involves a large open wound that can require a variety of treatments. The treatment course to remove the infection from Tara's finger required her to be hooked up to an IV for three hours to receive antibiotics on a weekly basis. After undergoing the first round of treatment, the wound on her finger continued to remain open and did not heal. When we met, the divorce attorney was going through her second round of antibiotics administered by IV. If the second treatment did not heal the infection, the next step would be to surgically clean out the wound, and if the infection worsened, her finger could end up having to be amputated.

Like most people, I have read stories about the flesh-eating bacteria, but this was my first encounter with someone who was fighting the infection. Rather than being afraid, I was intrigued to discover what could be done to help Tara's body to heal. I took my usual precautions right before the appointment and surrounded myself with a bubble of white light to extend God's protection around me during the session. And I did not practice my usual technique where I ask my client to place their hands on top of mine, palm to palm. Once we are sitting together I allow myself to breathe deeply and to turn to my intuition to ask it to reveal to me what I need to know about the person seated before me. I receive information in the form of clairaudience, which means I hear a word or phrase that directs me on how to begin the session. Finally, once an appointment with my client draws to a close, I do an energy release technique that involves me washing my hands with soap and water and verbally or silently stating that any energy that is not mine should be returned to the earth for the highest good for all involved. My releasing technique includes visualizing that energy is flowing from the top of my head all the way to the bottom of my feet and I imagine feeling it being returned to earth. Since Tara's circumstances were much different than any other client I had met with before, I decided to rely strictly on my internal senses to tell me what I needed to know to help her.

After quieting my mind and asking my intuition to direct me on what I needed to know for my session, one word came through loud and clear "anger." Immediately after hearing this intuitive insight, I looked at the large bandage on the middle finger of Tara's right hand, I asked if she thought it was significant that the virus attacked that particular finger. Most of us are familiar with what it means to "give someone the finger" when we are angry or upset. To clarify what I sensed intuitively, I asked Tara, "Do you use that finger much?"

"Not any more than my other ones," she replied.

For some reason, her words felt hollow to me, and I sensed intuitively this was a woman who had been angry for a long time.

There could be many reasons why the divorce attorney was angry. What I have found in my work is that whenever a person comes to see me who is angry, usually, the pattern has existed for such a long time that it can take a while to get to the root cause of what is bothering them. Due to the seriousness of the health concerns for Tara's finger, we did not have the luxury of time when it came to figuring out the underlying issue for her anger. Before the session ended, I knew Tara had been self-reliant and self-contained for so long that it would be difficult for her to allow herself to be vulnerable and tell me whatever had given her such a tough exterior.

As we talked, I asked Tara to describe the weekly treatment course of antibiotics she was receiving at the hospital. "I have to sit for three long hours while the medication is put in my arm by IV. It is a total waste of my time, so I try to plan my time and do something productive. Usually, I bring my checkbook in to pay my bills and work on the legal cases that need my attention. I am too busy at work to just sit and do nothing for three hours."

After listening carefully to her describe the treatment course, I told her that the first thing she needed to do was to abandon the belief that the antibiotics being infused in her body by IV were a waste of her time. From this point on, the most important thing in her life was to fully commit to her own healing if she wanted to avoid surgery or possibly even losing her finger. When she left that day, I gave her the following homework assignment:

1. Leave all busy work at home during the time that she received treatment and focus on her mind, body, heart and finger, setting the intention for all her cells, systems and organs to work with the medication to heal.
2. Silently tell her finger she loved it for 10 minutes, four times each day.
3. Each morning, set the intention that healing was her top priority.
4. Meditate at least four times a day on all her cells, systems and organs working together to direct healing to her finger.
5. Laugh as much as possible.

My approach in guiding Tara's healing was to introduce an infusion of loving thoughts in her mind, body and spirit as many times as possible. This was based on the need to engage all parts of her body on the crucially important job of healing. My perception on guiding a person to heal is a direct result of the startling research by Dr. Masaru Emoto in his book *The True Power of Water: Healing and Discovering Ourselves*. The Japanese doctor first became interested in water research in 1987, when he decided to dedicate himself to determining if water responded to positive words, phrases or music. This is what Dr. Emoto says about the information our bodies receive from water:

> *"The information can be either positive or negative. Since we are made up of 70% water, our body responds to the information we receive by the water we drink. When we get positive information from water, we*

become healthier. When we get negative information, we get sick."

Dr. Emoto's detailed research involved collecting water samples from all over the world, freezing the samples, painstakingly placing the frozen drops on slides, and viewing them under a high-powered microscope to determine the quality of the water crystals that were formed. He developed the hypothesis that water shows different shapes of crystals depending on the information it received. His revolutionary research proves that water responds to positive words and formed beautiful crystals. Dr. Emoto's findings are very significant since the average adult body is made up of 65% water.

My hope was that infusing Tara's finger with love, in addition to her fully committing for the first time to her own healing, would stimulate her body to fight the infection. It took only a few minutes of her sending love to the finger the first day in my office for the 63-year-old woman to tell me she could feel her finger tingling underneath the bandage.

Curiously enough, on the same night of our first session, a dream gave me valuable information to understanding the deep layer of pain that Tara was holding in her body.

After falling asleep quickly that same night, I had only been dozing for a couple of hours when I entered into an extremely violent dream that filled me with terror. The dream began with me walking down a dark street when a man suddenly appeared and started chasing me. While running as fast as I could, the man somehow managed to catch me and began to brutally beat me. The unknown male assailant was so strong and powerful that he slammed me on the ground, and I immediately knew that he intended to kill me. I made the decision to fight for my life and savagely ripped at the man's eyes and bit his hand. My attacker was momentarily caught off guard when I scratched him over his eye, giving me the opportunity to reach for his throat and start to choke him. The fight was so realistic that I consciously made the decision to kill my attacker rather than be killed. I saw with complete detail my hands wrapped around his throat as I tried to strangle the life out of him. The ferocity of my strength surprised my attacker and he realized our fight would go to the end. After that, the man gave me a hard shove and ran away. I woke up from this all too-realistic attack trembling, as my mind tried to shake off the physical and emotional effects of having been involved in such a violent fight.

Unable to sleep, I made myself a cup of tea to calm my nerves. As my breathing started to return to normal, my mind kept flashing back to the extremely frightening moment when my hands were around my attacker's neck. To help me grasp the details, I wrote everything down in my dream journal with the plan to review it when my mind was calmer.

The next morning, I made the decision to turn to my intuition to determine the underlying reason for my dream. Realizing that I needed to calm myself to be able to fully listen to my intuition, I decided to meditate.

Meditation is an effective practice that allows you to connect with your intuition. Whenever I begin a meditation, my first step is to surround myself with the light of God's love. For me, I visualize a white bubble of light and ask to be guided with the highest good to the information I need. Once I feel myself slip into a state of inner peace, my mind completely disconnecting from the busyness of the physical world, I ask the question that needs to be answered. Once you pose your question, it takes dedicated practice to notice how your senses respond when you make a request for information. There are times when no answer surfaces. What I have learned is that, like many people, my "aha" moments often come to me in the shower. Setting the intention for the information that I need, and relaxing, invariably allows me to hear my intuition.

The question I asked was if my dream was connected to the woman with the flesh-eating bacteria. It was only a minute later that I got a definite "yes," and I was certain my fateful dream would be the starting point of our next session together.

My second session with the 63-year-old attorney began with me asking, "When were you attacked?" I watched the woman's face tighten to the point of forming lines around her mouth before she responded. Suddenly, I saw a slight flicker in her eyes, which I took as a sign she would open up and tell me what had happened to her. Tara talked non-stop for the next hour recalling how she was brutally attacked 10 years earlier. It had happened late one night after the divorce attorney met some friends for drinks and she was unable to find a cab. Tara decided to walk the three or four blocks home when a man suddenly came up from behind and grabbed the purse she had over her shoulder. A brutal fight ensued. My client described herself "as fighting for her life," with the struggle finally ending after she decided to try to kill her attacker by gripping her hands around his throat and squeezing until he weakened. Her assailant eventually ran off. She filed a police report but no one was ever charged with the attack.

After hearing all this, I strongly believed that Tara could heal the flesh-eating bacteria without having surgery. Even as she told me of the attack, the strong-willed woman never cried. She shared with me the details of the attack very calmly, but I knew that the memory of this brutal, life-threatening experience was lodged deeply in her mind and heart.

Sharing with her my own dream, I sensed my biggest challenge would be to help Tara release the fight or flight response that she has maintained since being attacked. A fight or flight response can best be described as a person's reaction to what they perceive to be a threatening situation. If you think that running is the best option to ward off an attack, this may be your only choice of action. When Tara was attacked, she wisely decided that fighting was the only option to ensure her survival. In addition to focusing on loving her finger each day, her homework assignment included being aware of any circumstances which made her want to "give the finger" to someone, and then not to do it under any circumstances.

It made me feel good to know that Tara was listening when she shared with me a recent incident: When another driver cut her off in traffic, she suppressed the desire to give him the finger. Tara's decision to heal the flesh-eating bacteria was causing her to examine her emotions like never before.

After the third session with me, Tara's doctor was very pleased to see that the wound was finally healing. She finished the final round of antibiotics without any further problems.

Being able to heal the flesh-eating bacteria alerted Tara of the need to carefully monitor whenever the emotion of anger emerged for her. At our final session, the divorce attorney surprised me when she admitted that one of the unexpected benefits of working with me was that her relationships with her friends improved. People she had known for many years finally revealed that Tara's need for control had made it difficult for them to interact with her. She has vowed to be more peaceful and Tara promised to completely break the habit of giving the finger to anyone from this point on.

Tara's decision to tap into her power to heal is the same power everyone has whenever they are facing a health challenge.

Here are the steps to take to connect with your own ability to heal:

1. Set the intention each day that your need to heal is your top priority.

2. Offer prayers and talk directly to the organ involved.

3. Express your prayers in the past tense, professing that you are grateful for your complete healing.

4. Be willing to explore any trauma that has impacted your life.

5. Do not let a negative event destroy the balance and direction in your life.

When a 5-year-old intelligent little girl from Baltimore first realized her gift of intuition, she used it to keep herself safe. Consuella "Connie" Newton, 82, a retired educator, remembers with vivid detail how her perceptive abilities let her know the best time to go to the grocery store to protect her from girl bullies in her neighborhood. Sometimes calling herself a "natural" intuitive, Newton hid her gift for many years to appease her very cautious and religious family. A near-death experience changed all that and compelled her to embrace her abilities to guide and teach others how to tap into their inner consciousness.

Growing up as a highly intuitive child caused many awkward moments in her family. Without trying, Newton knew when people were going to die and she also became acutely aware when someone was lying. It was hard to keep the bright child from blurting these things out.

Newton's great aunt kept the little girl on a tight leash and enforced the standing rule for her to "keep her mouth shut" and not to tell anyone about her secret. This was based on her family's belief that if her classmates knew, Newton would not have any friends because their parents would not allow their children to play with her. The family line of intuitive intelligence extended to both parents of this highly gifted child. Her father had the gift of second sight, giving him the ability to see into the future, and it took many years before Newton's mother was comfortable in recognizing and developing her own intuitive gift.

There was no formal education for the type of invisible energy that Newton connected with from a very early age. Her intuition works differently from the mundane way of getting a "hunch." **She accesses her internal guardian in a variety of ways:**

- **Clairaudience:** The ability to hear things outside of the normal range of perception.

- **Clairvoyance:** Clear vision; a kind of extrasensory perception that reveals things that are hidden.

- **Clairsentience:** A form of extra-sensory perception wherein a person acquires psychic knowledge primarily by feeling.

- **Auric perceptions**: An energy field that is visible around people and or places.

- **Telepathy:** Hearing directions to safe places and subjects to teach.

Receiving a constant flow of multi-sensory perceptions as a small child must have been overwhelming. Despite having a complicated "inner world," Connie was an excellent straight-A student who was eager to learn, knowing early on that she wanted to be a teacher. It could be said that Newton's education involved her going to two schools simultaneously. One was in the segregated neighborhood she attended as a "Negro" girl in Baltimore, and the other was where Connie learned to recognize the invisible perceptions going on inside of her. The little girl had the remarkable ability of being able to "turn off" her perceptions when needed.

The highly intuitive girl grew into a young woman who married and achieved her goal of becoming a secondary school teacher while continuing to live by her family's rules. That all changed close to 50 years ago when Newton was scheduled to undergo routine gynecological surgery at the esteemed Johns Hopkins Hospital in Baltimore, Maryland. She was told the operation would only last an hour, but minutes before the surgery, while she was lying on a gurney, she heard the voice of her guardian angel say, in Newton's words, that "there would be difficulty with my operation and that I had been destined to die, and that another family member would pass instead. I responded that I did not want to go yet because I had done nothing worthwhile for mankind."

After hearing these words, Newton could not shake the feeling of apprehension, despite her doctor's reassurance that everything would be okay.

Later in the operating room, Newton viewed her own operation from the invisible ringside seat from the top of the room. The retired educator recalled watching her doctor down to the acute detail of seeing him jerk his hands from the surgical field when she developed a breathing problem. Newton's doctor was shocked when in ICU, she told him word-for-word what he said during her long three-hour operation.

Waking up in ICU after going through this near-death experience, Newton became aware for the first time of her gift of auric perception and her ability to see the auric energy fields surrounding the nurses and doctors who attended her. (An aura is a field of subtle, luminous radiating light that surrounds a person like a halo or bubble.)

The auric energy field Newton saw was so bright that she viewed her nurse bathed in a beautiful blue light. But when a doctor came in who did not reflect the same healing energy, Newton, a strong-willed Scorpio, refused to allow him to touch her. After two long and very difficult days in ICU, Newton returned home to embrace the work that she was meant to do.

This experience served as the catalyst that persuaded Newton to inform her family of her decision to work with her gifts. This led to Newton devoting 43 years to teaching how higher-consciousness living enhances day-to-day life.

In 1976, Newton created a unique learning experience known as Integrated Awareness Technique (IA), to help others tap into their consciousness and use it as a finely sharpened tool that can be accessed in a moment's notice. In 2000, she expanded her teaching by developing Perception Awareness Technique (PAT), a three-day program in which she trains others to teach small groups how to utilize their intuition to make better life choices. She is also the originator of a unique healing technique known as Soma Pi. This is a preventive healing force that is used by certified practitioners all over the country.

What is even more amazing about all this is that Newton's classes, workshops, conferences and webinars have filled with thousands of eager students through the years, despite her never advertising or marketing her programs. Students are drawn to her teachings from as far away as Europe, South America, Canada and Egypt. And there is no formal structure surrounding Newton's learning experiences. Attendees are not required to join an organization or pay membership fees.

Newton has touched thousands of lives through her appearances on television and radio in addition to being a popular guest lecturer and workshop leader across the country at colleges, universities and symposiums. Her book, *The Inner Quest*, was nominated for the Georgia Author of the Year Award. Newton was also a regular featured columnist for the now defunct International World Times newspaper, under the byline "Thoughtful Insight." The esteemed speaker and educator describes how she learned to rely on her internal guardian in her life:

> *"My intuition is as natural as breathing for me. It is*
> *an aspect of my everyday life that I use for everything.*
> *This wonderful connective energy has always led me*
> *in the right direction."*

It takes only a few minutes of talking to the impeccably dressed and gifted intuitive to sense her deep commitment to guide and teach others how to expand their inner consciousness. Asked why many men and women are blocked from achieving success, the retired educator indicates it is because they are not being taught how to use their intuition:

> *"Abiding by only the strict ritualistic teaching of organized religion, we don't look inside for the answers we need. When people are alert to their intuition, they will have less heartbreak. Individuals often overrule their intuition because they get caught up in the trappings and not the core essence of the person. It does not matter if you are Black, White, Hispanic or Asian. All of us are stronger than we realize. Everyone has a wide range of opportunities. And we can reach beyond the confines of the limitations of where they are now. All of us must always have goals, be aware of what you are becoming so that you can climb the ladder of higher consciousness and take someone with you."*

A graduate of Morgan State University, Newton is listed in Cambridge Who's Who and has done post-graduate work in speech pathology at Loyola College in Baltimore. She has also been affiliated with a psychologist, Dr. William Parker, in the work of prayer therapy for many years. Her expansive knowledge has involved sponsoring tours in which she has taken large groups of people to Egypt, Australia, New Zealand, China and Tibet.

As a senior citizen, Newton has not slowed down in her passion for teaching higher consciousness. Her son, Derek Newton, is her trusted technical advisor on all her projects while her husband of 59 years, Jim Newton, a retired oil executive, remains her staunchest supporter and advocate.

PART III
CHOICES

Ask her about the gun.

That is the shocking insight my intuition revealed to me in one of my very first appointments when I started seeing clients professionally in 2006. Hearing those words made my brain spin and had me wondering whether I was crazy trying to use my inner wisdom to help others. Staying in a perpetual state of panic was not possible that day because I had a new client seated in my office. Finally, in desperation, I decided to check in again with my intuitive process to see if I heard the same cryptic message.

Waiting and trusting what is received when I enter into silence to request information I need is the most significant part of my work. Despite my own internal anxiety over the intuitive insight I received on my client, "Kelly," an attractive, tall 32-year-old woman, appeared to be very relaxed and at ease as the cryptic message kept going round and round in my brain.

In many ways, not owning up to my skill was like hiding in a closet from whom I really am. The person who persuaded me to stop hiding was my mentor and friend, Kurt Hill, founder of Holistic Health Practice in Chicago. The two of us met when I scheduled an appointment to receive bodywork from the highly respected energy and vibrational healer. (Vibrational medicine is also known as a form of alternative medicine that is also called energy medicine and energy healing. It is based on the concept that a healer can channel healing into the person who needs to recover from an ailment.)

After I entered his office, Kurt said in his rich baritone voice, "You are probably one of the most intuitive people I've had walk through my door. Why aren't you doing your work?" He had no way of knowing that the question he posed to me was the same one I had been struggling with for the previous two years. His question threw me for a loop and I really did not know how to respond. Finally, the only answer I could think to tell him was my need to support myself and be able to send my daughter to college.

A few emails later, the two of us met for lunch and to my surprise, the man who has become one of my most trusted friends invited me to join his practice. Luckily for me, the office he assigned me to work in was right next door to his, making it easy for me to walk only a short distance and seek his advice.

My decision to turn to Kurt for help required me to interrupt him during an appointment he had with a client. When he answered the door, I quickly said, "I've got a big problem," and shared with him the cryptic intuitive insight that kept coming up. My words had a significant impact on him by the way his thick eyebrows shot up underneath the large, black square-shaped eyeglasses he always wears.

Quickly stepping back into his office, Kurt excused himself to his client and the two of us went into my office. After introducing Kelly to Kurt, we exchanged casual conversation for a couple of minutes before I found the courage to ask her, "What does a gun have to do with your appointment with me today?"

Without hesitation, the 32-year-old woman told us that she had been thinking about killing her estranged husband. Her words hung in the air for a full minute until I found the nerve to ask if she had a gun with her that day. When she nodded "yes," my mind went entirely blank.

Kurt took over the questioning at that point, and we found out Kelly was licensed to carry a firearm in her job as a law enforcement officer. He wisely asked the officer to put her service revolver in the trash can next to my chair and told her that it would be in our reception area where she could retrieve it on her way out. Right before leaving my office with my trash can in his hand, Kurt winked at me, and I knew intuitively this was his way of letting me know to trust myself.

Alone now again with my client, my heart was pounding in my chest, and all I could think to do was to pray. Taking a deep breath, I went deep into my heart and invited God along with every angel, power of light and spiritual master to be present and assist me in serving at the highest level. There is no other way to say what happened after that, but I felt a subtle energy shift in the room and sensed a loving supportive life force that stayed with me during the entire session. Feeling more comfortable for the first time, I allowed myself to completely trust my intuition in whatever it revealed.

As we talked, I followed my hunch and asked Kelly about her childhood. "Were you a happy child?" I asked.

The female officer continued her pattern of being extremely open and revealed a painful and tremendously difficult childhood where she suffered unspeakable terror that included verbal, physical, emotional and even sexual abuse by various family members. She never cried as she described her life story to me, and instinctively I knew that she was a woman who survived by being strong and fiercely independent.

Reflecting on Kelly's painful past, I heard myself say to her, "Allow me to apologize to you from the Universe. You did not deserve what happened to you." And I went on say that I was in awe of her courage and strength and wondered to myself if I could have done the same thing if the situation was reversed.

After that, a slight smile lit up Kelly's face and she told me the turning point in her life came when she made the decision to become a police officer. After graduating from the Chicago Police Academy with top grades, the female officer attracted the attention of the brass and was recruited to be a member of an elite drug team. The job required intensive specialized training to work undercover to infiltrate the dangerous world of drug dealers. As the only African-American woman on the team, Kelly's addition to the department gave them access to investigations in diverse areas that they could not do with a team that consisted of 98% white male officers. From day one, the racially segregated team made no secret of the fact that they disliked having a black female working with them. Every day, Kelly faced an extremely stressful work environment; first, from the dangerous drug deals she participated in; second, from the racial taunts and insults from the white male officers. While hearing this, it hit me how ironic it was for Kelly to have to depend on those same officers to keep her safe. Trying to block out the high-stress levels, she sought comfort in relationships with men who repeated her dysfunctional family pattern. Without strong interpersonal relationships at work or at home, it is no surprise that the officer ignored her intuition and married a man she knew would not make a good husband.

Kelly's husband moved into the three-bedroom custom home purchased through her strong work ethic. Additionally, she carried the burden of long overtime hours on her highly stressful job, a small business she started in her home, and security details for an elite clientele. Less than a year into the marriage, the couple was having non-stop arguments. Things worsened after the birth of their child, who was born premature and required hospitalization in a neonatal care unit. When their infant son came home, Kelly was faced with the overwhelming load of single-handedly providing for his delicate care. During this difficult period, it was not unusual for Kelly's husband to come home from work and provoke nasty arguments between them. When the arguments became physical, the officer finally told her husband to get out of her house. When she came to see me, the two were in a bitter legal fight, going through a divorce in which her husband was demanding half of the house's worth for which Kelly worked so hard.

Faced with a constant fight for survival at work and at home, it was no surprise to me that the officer would think that violence was her only option.

I am convinced that Kelly's appointment with me that day represented a turning point for both of us. A turning point can best be described as a moment in which you make a conscious decision or intention to take an action that will forever change your life.

One of the best descriptions of how to approach a turning point is written by Gregg Braden in his book *The Turning Point: Creating Resilience in a Time of Extremes*. **The author describes the three choices everyone faces in these moments:**

1. We recognize the turning point and embrace it; the new information becomes the reason to think and act differently.

2. The turning point is rejected; when a person rejects what is really going on, they believe it is possible to think and live the way they did in the past and go about business as usual.

3. The power of the turning point is ignored.

One choice missing from Braden's list in dealing with a turning point is our ability to communicate with our heart to empower us to know the best choice for us to make. Our hearts are involved in much more than just pumping blood through our arteries, veins, capillaries and organs. Science has proven that our hearts and brains are always in a state of communication. Developing heart-based communication has the power to change our thinking and ultimately our lives. It was easy to sense Kelly's feelings of anger, rage and even hatred towards her husband, and I knew the only way to shift her thinking was to get her to listen to her heart.

I started by asking her to tell me about the future goals she had for her son. The devoted mother smiled as she described the dreams, hopes and desires she had for her only child. By then, our appointment had long exceeded the hour we were originally scheduled. It seemed as if we were in an invisible energy connection that allowed things to flow the way they needed to.

As she talked about her son, I noticed Kelly's voice became softer as she shared with me her desire for him to be a good student and have the opportunity to have the simple things she did not have as a child—a nice home, the ability to make friends and have them visit, and to be completely encouraged and supported in going to college. The 32-year-old mother spoke from her heart, and this opened the doorway for me to discuss one of the most powerful laws in the universe: the Law of Cause and Effect. This law teaches that for every action there is an equal reaction. This law directly connects to the underlying belief in karma. Karma is the belief that our mistakes and how we treat others affects our future. Essentially, karma, like the Law of Cause and Effect, offers us the ability to learn life's lessons. What this means is that we cannot escape from our mistakes, especially when we harm others. Each of us has the opportunity to exercise free will and make choices that allow us to create a good life.

As we approached the end of what had become a two-hour session, I told Kelly that whatever decision she made would determine whether the dreams she had for her son would become true or place him at risk of being raised by the very people who had brutally abused her. I said to her, "The most meaningful way to show love to your son is by not destroying your own life." After my final statement, I noticed a subtle energy shift in Kelly as she nodded slightly.

My session with Kelly took place nearly eight years ago and it is forever etched in my mind as the turning point in my work. This was my introductory lesson on the power of acting on a hunch and following the invisible signal that leads me in my work with my clients. Clearly, there was an invisible hand at play in our meeting that day.

Unbeknownst to me, the choice I made to follow Kurt's advice and do the work my inner wisdom had been urging me to do for two years would lead to one of the greatest opportunities to learn what it means to really trust my intuition. Both Kelly and I that day were playing a part in the mystical theatre that was directing our lives. It took years for me to have complete understanding of why this all happened the way it did.

As the final draft was being reviewed for this book, a wonderful synchronicity occurred in which Kelly and I saw each other. It took only a few minutes after we hugged before I asked about her son. He is a teenager now and is a good student and athlete. She is, as I expected, a very proud mother. Talking with her, I sensed in Kelly the same fighter spirit that gave her the strength to survive the unthinkable pain of being molested, as well as a bitter divorce. She continues to be a woman who is a warrior and sued the DEA for the racial and sexual harassment she went through on the job. On appeal, she was awarded a $750,000 settlement. Kelly has written her own book that is a source of pride and strength to anyone who must overcome tremendous challenges in their lives. Currently, she is in negotiation with a producer to turn her life story into a movie.

Kelly's story serves as a source of inspiration to anyone who feels that they are trapped and have no options other than violence. There are always consequences to our actions. The only way we can change our external circumstances is to change on an internal level. A turning point in our lives gives us the magnificent opportunity to create a new way to deal with any challenge.

Here are the steps to explore and understand what to do when you reach a turning point in your life:

1. Know yourself and get professional help before you become

overwhelmed.

2. Embrace the belief that your life and world are changing for the better.

3. Listen to your heart and recognize what you care most about in your life.

4. Maintain a spiritual practice and pray for guidance, direction and wisdom every day.

5. Exercise on a regular basis. Even 10-15 minutes a day will help to release endorphins in your mind to be able to think optimistically.

6. Identify your core values. The answers will help clarify what you need to do when facing a difficult decision.

The life of Kurt A. Hill, Sr., was forever altered in 1992 when he was a passenger in a near-fatal car accident. While he walked away from the crash with no physical injuries, the experience transformed the CEO of a small plastics company from being singularly focused on building his business to a life of helping others to heal.

Hill, African American, was 41 years old at the time of the crash and was driven to achieve success for the company he painstakingly grew for eight years with 10 employees. The CEO went to work each day proudly wearing his corporate uniform: a Brooks Brothers suit and briefcase close by his side, always ready for any business opportunity that came up.

Hill started his business in the late 1980s, an exciting period to be an MBE (Minority Business Enterprise), with the doorway finally open for minorities to be able to compete for lucrative government and corporate contracts. Eager to prove his company's worth, Hill put his heart and soul into preparing for a business meeting in Detroit, Michigan. Staying up for two nights, the tight schedule required the CEO to drive from Chicago to Detroit. Feeling exhausted, Hill wisely asked his vice president and friend, K.C. Khalid Sheriff, to do the driving. Just minutes after they hit the road, he pushed the passenger seat into a recline position, crossed his arms and quickly fell asleep. Hill had only been asleep for less than an hour when their trip took an unexpected turn. A rainstorm had started and his VP shook him awake screaming, "We are in TROUBLE—our brakes are out."

Hill was not wearing a seat belt and he described watching in slow

financial counseling.

As his practice grew, Hill was drawn to include spiritual counseling as part of his work and at the age of 55, he enrolled in Chicago Theological Seminary. He took night classes at the seminary majoring in Theology and Seminary. His studies included doing a hospital internship at night in which he attended to patients suffering from terminal illness. He did all this while handling his usual client load of treating 10-12 people per day and sleeping only three to four hours per night.

It is hard to imagine the man who started his practice being known as "the healer's healer" slowing down in his work. Hill, now 65 years old, continues on his quest for knowledge to treat clients with the most advanced form of healing. During his over twenty-year quest for knowledge, he has become a licensed massage therapist and specialist in cranio-sacral therapy with credentials in vibrational medicine, spiritual counseling and MYO trigger point therapy. He is also the founder of Advanced Psychosomatic Character Therapy and is a candidate for a master's in psychology from the Adler School of Professional Psychology.

In addition to his constant quest for education, Hill credits his life partner Sara Davenport and his three children, Kurt A. Hill, Jr., Erik Hill and Kaila Hill, as a constant source of love and support.

Hill's prestigious work includes writing and publishing his first book, *Call of the Dragon: Behold the Pleroma* in 2014.

One client who comes in regularly to see me is a 41-year-old IT specialist named Jacob "Jake" Rice. He is consciously aware of his intuition, and this plays a big role in his ability to not only find jobs but also to frequently be promoted with sizeable pay raises. He works in the highly competitive area of search engine optimization (SEO), and is often pursued for job opportunities. He is also the only client who has been able to visualize the energy surrounding my intuitive process.

During one of our first appointments, Jake identified my intuitive process by drawing a silhouette of my body, and followed that by quickly drawing three circles surrounding me, the biggest one being white, the middle one yellow and the circle closest to my body as blue. To this day, I still have that random sketch Jake drew for me.

What amazes me most about Jake is his willingness to embrace negotiating with his peers on everything. I have noticed this in many of my male clients - they like to plan upcoming negotiations for both their personal and professional lives. It is fascinating to witness the process men go through to prepare for this. They see it as a game.

To start, men tend to operate in a bantering conversation mode with all their co-workers. This is a normal part of their day-to-day interactions, and they easily go through a conversation not overly concerned with all the comments that are made. The key to this strategy is that the men I talk with are actively engaged in collecting data from these random talks. Essentially, they operate in the same mode as detectives do when they are investigating a case. Jake told me that he stores the information he gathers, laying the groundwork for future negotiations.

Meanwhile, he continued to meet with me, where he recorded my intuitive insights in a small notebook. Jake believed our meetings gave him a favorable edge in achieving his compensation goals. This is the major difference between my male and female clients. Women will often not pursue negotiating with the same dedication and gusto as their male counterparts. Studies show that women are just as good at negotiating as men—except when it comes to negotiating for ourselves. We speak up for our kids and family members, yet when it comes to looking for ourselves, we often downplay our value and worth.

Whenever a woman is planning a serious negotiation, either professionally or personally, she needs to prepare the same way athletes do and train for the meeting by developing a winning strategy that includes imaging what we want to create in our lives. Whenever we emotionally embrace the future outcome we desire, we are raising our consciousness. Dr. Joe Dispenza, author of *You Are the Placebo: Making Your Mind Matter*, has this to say about operating in the visible field of consciousness:

> " . . . if you observe yourself in a particular new future that was different from your past, expected the reality to occur, and then emotionally embraced the outcome, you'd be—for a moment—living in the future reality, and you'd be conditioning your body to believe that it was in the present moment."

During our prep sessions, we performed a series of vision exercises in which Jake imaged all the details about talking to his boss. In other words, he mentally rehearsed what he wanted to take place and fully connected with his emotions to feel excitement and enthusiasm for the upcoming meeting. As scientific research has proven, by actively using our imagination, our body registers the same physical reaction as an actual experience.

Jake's visioning including focusing on developing a powerful list of specific successes he had achieved on various projects. In the three years we had worked together, the IT specialist has been promoted each year and received substantial pay increases, so he had an abundance of good material to work with.

The average person prepares for a salary negotiation by reviewing their past performance reports, analyzing the salaries of their peers as well as comparable jobs in their industry, and putting together a list of successful projects. When we combine the factual data with our ability to tap into our senses, feelings, thoughts and imagination, we are operating at the highest level of free will. Scientists have proven that when we use our minds to imagine, while embracing our emotions, our body responds to the elevated energy of our consciousness.

It is all too common for us to live in the same emotional state every day. We are much more powerful than we realize and each of us can choose to reprogram ourselves to feel deeply about our lives. By doing this, we are creating a new state of being that strengthens and expands our intuition.

As his big meeting approached, Jake continued his pattern of hanging out with his peers and mentoring those who needed additional training. If the IT specialist sensed that a person on his team did not have the toolset needed for a project, he used that as a teaching moment for everyone involved. His management style involved frequent "learning breaks," where Jake would ask one person on his team to demonstrate the newly acquired toolset immediately after the impromptu learning session. Then he called on others to demonstrate the technique on subsequent days so that the entire team completely grasped the assigned task. As you might expect, Jake's team members are also easily promoted. He instills self-confidence and a love for learning that makes everyone want to perform at their highest level. My sense is that Jake's cutting edge skills will lead him to soon write a bestselling book on search engine optimization.

The creative energy Jake radiates, I believe, is directly connected to his being completely honest with himself on all levels. He is openly gay and recently married his long-time partner. Coming to grips with his sexuality was not easy. When Jake came out to his mother at age 22, she told him to move out. Despite how she treated him, Jake and his friends organized and maintained a vigil at his mom's bedside when she was in intensive care due to a life-changing injury. Even now, he continues to maintain close contact with his younger siblings in the household to help guide and direct their futures. He defines what it means to truly release the past by funneling his energy into creative pursuits.

Success does not happen by accident. People who are open to new ideas and concepts will practice mental rehearsals as part of their preparation process.

Here are the steps to creating your own mental rehearsal:

1. Quiet your mind.

2. Set the intention for what you want to create.

3. Visualize the desired outcome and be aware of all of the thoughts, feelings and emotions you will experience when your dream manifests.

4. Be grateful for the moment in consciousness.

5. Observe and pay attention to the positive emotions that emerge inside of you, and commit to experiencing them in your daily life on a regular basis.

Men hide their insecurities beneath locker room camaraderie and sports metaphors. Our boyfriends, partners, husbands, fathers, uncles, nephews, cousins, friends, brothers, sons and grandfathers are all taught to be strong from a very early age.

The two core messages men learn that serve as the underlying foundation for their need to be strong are: Big boys do not cry and take it like a man. These messages shape how men think and act in all areas of their lives.

Many of my male clients tell me that they received their first verbal messages to be strong while they were still quite young.

Men react to the pressure of being strong by refusing to acknowledge their doubts, fears and insecurities to themselves and others. This is one of the underlying factors why many men avoid going to the doctor.

In the book, *Reclaiming Sex & Intimacy After Prostate Cancer*, author Jeffery Albaugh, Ph.D., who is a 25-year advanced urology clinical nurse specialist, cites two fundamental reasons why men are not inclined to discuss health matters: Males are not as health conscious as women, and they consider health matters to be private. Albaugh says men often minimize health concerns and exist in the mindset that "if they do not think about it, it does not exist." The author cites the three most feared words for a man to hear are "digital rectal exam."

All of my first-time clients are asked to complete an intake form that requests the date of their last health exam. It is not unusual for men to leave this question blank. It is only after I gently probe my male clients that more than half will admit not having been in a doctor's office for at least two years. One client, "Ralph," a 41-year-old married attorney with two young children, had not seen a doctor in over five years when he came in to see me for the first time. The reasons he cited were work demands and too much time spent socializing with his clients.

My intuitive sense was that Ralph was reckless in other ways besides not taking care of his health. Furthermore, after discussing the socializing responsibilities of his career, the father of two admitted to consuming an excessive amount of alcohol. Ralph said that during social outings with his clients, he stops counting his drinks after seven cocktails. It took some convincing to get the 41-year-old attorney to accept that his drinking excessively was not only placing his own life at risk, but also having an effect on the career he valued so much. And it jeopardized the future of his family.

After our session, Ralph scheduled a physical examination and sailed through his tests with flying colors. He was grateful not to have any health problems. Once he understood the consequences of his actions, he decided to abstain from alcohol for 30 days. After achieving that goal, he decided to cut his alcohol consumption in half. When we followed up after our initial session, I asked Ralph how his wife reacted to the lifestyle changes he had recently made. It turns out his wife did not have a chance to react since Ralph kept news of the exam and the results to himself until after all the test results came back fine. This pattern of keeping secrets about health is very common with men.

Even men who are diligent in getting regular health exams will often not share their results with anyone, even their own spouses. The core message men receive of "always being strong" plays a big factor in whether they are being completely open when they go in for a doctor's appointment. Because men tend to keep their health private, it takes a major change in their body for them to admit what is going on.

This rang true for "Bob," a high-powered, 63-year-old executive who came to see me when he was having difficulty breathing. He was under the care of his primary care physician for treatment of hypertension and mild asthma, and he always got regular physical exams. The first thing that I sensed intuitively in our initial appointment was that my client was an expert at "telling half-truths." It took a couple of sessions before Bob finally owned up to the fact that even while he was going to the doctor regularly, he was only occasionally taking his hypertension medication, and preferred to treat himself with vitamins and herbs.

Noticing Bob's shallow breathing while he was talking, I advised him to see a respiratory specialist for a second opinion. Initially he balked at my advice, but he called back two or three days later to tell me he had been admitted to the hospital. The respiratory specialist correctly diagnosed his breathing discomfort as the beginning stage of congestive heart failure, with fluid buildup around his lungs and heart.

Bob had a hard time accepting that his failure to take his hypertension medication was the primary cause for the fluid buildup. He recovered fully and now practices complete disclosure with his doctor.

There are a number of conditions everyone faces as we age, including heart disease, high cholesterol and diabetes. These are all diseases that must be carefully monitored so that more serious problems do not develop. Men must go to the doctor on a regular basis and be truthful about their symptoms and whatever at-home treatments they are administering.

A spot on his lung is what brought in a 60-year-old advertising salesman "Kevin" to see me for the first time. He looked fidgety and admitted to smoking his entire life. What he did not tell me until later was the pattern of negative self-talk that existed in his life as a result of staying in an unhappy 25-year marriage. As I connected with the tall advertising salesman on an intuitive level, I asked specifically for the spiritual connection to be revealed as the client requested. Allowing myself to tune in to Kevin's spiritual journey, I had one of the most unusual insights I have ever received. My intuition told me the following: "This soul has been abandoned and neglected for so long that it would be easier to leave the confines of this body than to stay and work with this one."

Hearing these words shocked me, and I immediately stopped Kevin's reading and asked him what had he been saying to himself? Looking me directly in the eye, the salesmen told me, "I have been saying for the last two years I do not care if I live or die."

The will to live is the most powerful energetic field each of us must embrace on a daily basis, whether we are facing a crisis in our life or not. This is one area that we cannot compromise on in our conscious thoughts. Every suicide is not recorded as a suicide, as there are many instances in which people "will" themselves to die.

The creator of the Integrated Awareness Technique, Consuella Newton, strongly suggests daily use of the affirmation, "I will to live," especially when there is a risk of life or death. Each of us is capable of daily self-empowerment by affirming this statement to ourselves, to God and to the universe.

For many men, it is only when they are facing a medical crisis that they are willing to disclose the true nature of their personal problems. In Kevin's case, he existed in a name-only marriage for more than 25 years. Both parties were openly hostile to each other and slept in separate bedrooms. The couple has two adult children and maintained separate relationships with them. The family had not celebrated a holiday together in many years.

Shortly after our first appointment, Kevin was diagnosed with lung cancer. He was told that his condition was terminal, and while there was an initial effort made for him to receive chemotherapy, he died within two months of the diagnosis. There is no doubt in my mind that Kevin's pattern of negative self-talk (which was a direct result of staying in a very unhappy marriage) and smoking for over 30 years both played significant parts in his death.

Even while he was nearing transition, Kevin and his wife did not heal the anger that existed between them. He talked openly that the biggest regret of his life was that he should have walked away from the marriage years before. I believe that making good decisions about what makes you happy in your life is just as important as going to the doctor and getting regular health exams.

In addition to health concerns, facing a major decision is the second reason that males often want to talk to me. That happened with a 27-year-old engineer, "Aaron," who worked in the building where I live. A wonderful synchronicity occurred when we ran into each other when I was heading for a luncheon meeting. He offered me a ride and shortly after I got in his car, Aaron told me about a great job offer he had received. He went on and on about the large sum of money that was being offered and how this would make things easier for his family. Staying aware, I noticed a subtle energy shift when he talked about the "great job offer." In other words, something did not feel right inside of me.

To confirm my hunch, I asked Aaron to pull over to allow me to do a quick intuitive reading on his job opportunity. What came through loud and clear was that the company did not have the funds to pay him the fantastic salary he mentioned. I conveyed this to him and urged Aaron to thoroughly examine the financial stability of his potential employer before leaving his current job.

Unfortunately, Aaron did not address the concerns I raised with him until after turning in his resignation. When he went to the office to talk with the person who made the job offer, Aaron finally asked questions about the financial state of the company. The man he spoke with "shrugged his shoulders" and "would not look him in the eye," all the while telling him verbally "everything was fine in the financial department." Aaron said he got a sickening feeling in his stomach during their conversation. The next day he received a phone call from another company official who said the position he was offered could not be funded since the firm was in bankruptcy. Aaron's intuition was clearly warning him things would not turn out well when he finally asked the questions that needed to be answered before he resigned.

Paying attention to your body's internal reaction to the non-verbal clues of others is one of the most valuable tools to help men and women think more intuitively. The excitement Aaron felt about being able to provide a better living for his family is what led him to hastily respond to the job offer without checking things out. In addition, when making his decision, the father of two failed to fully examine the pros and cons of the position where he had worked successfully for three years. This young man was earning union wages in his current job, and everyone Aaron worked with liked and respected him. His employer even allowed him to work flexible hours to be able to pick up his children from school when needed.

As you can imagine, Aaron was very angry with himself for not heeding the intuitive insight I shared with him. He admitted the big salary that was promised would have drastically improved his family's life, and this caused him to completely ignore my advice.

One of the most challenging experiences men face is when they make a mistake, especially when it impacts the safety and protection of their families. Many of the men I talk with beat themselves up for long periods over past errors. One critical factor that often limits many men from making wise decisions is that many of their choices are based solely on finances. This is not unusual since most men are not comfortable with talking or even considering the emotional aspect of any choice they are facing. When men focus only on the financial details concerning a decision, they place themselves at a big disadvantage and often make mistakes.

Aaron's mistake made him realize how grateful he was for the two women who mean the most to him: his wife and his mother. They both provided complete support as the family worked together to face this challenge. He has found another job and it has taken Aaron two years to slowly start to reach the salary he walked away from.

The underlying need for men to be strong also makes it difficult for them to seek outside counsel when they have a problem. And when they do seek advice, this does not always ensure they will follow it.

This was the case with "David," a 34-year-old single teacher who came to see me because his dating relationships lasted no more than a few months. The teacher, who has a master's degree, had no trouble finding women to date, but if the relationship hit a rough spot, it was commonplace for him to walk away rather than try to work things out. My client admitted to this without the slightest hint of guilt or remorse about his behavior. When I questioned whether he thought his actions were hurtful, David replied that he "did not like drama, and it was easier to just walk away."

It surprised me when I sensed intuitively that David's hurtful actions were not based on his being afraid to make a commitment. Rather he feared repeating the same pattern and choosing the wrong woman to be his wife. To the educator's credit, after coming to see me, David was open to changing his dating pattern. His willingness to change his life led him to pursue a relationship with a woman he met through a friend. The two dated for over a year, and they clicked so well that each of them had keys to the other's home. At some point, David admitted to becoming bored in the relationship and chose to revert to his old pattern. He simply stopped returning his girlfriend's phone calls and being around whenever she came by his house. Discussing the consequences of his actions, David believed that by handling things this way, he would not have to deal with the unpleasantness of ending the relationship. After a couple of months passed, his old girlfriend called and invited him to attend her company's outing at a large outdoor amusement park. Knowing how David treated the woman, I suggested that he pass on attending the event. He was persuaded by the lure of an all-expense-paid fun day at the amusement park and went anyway.

Shortly after they arrived at the venue, David was shocked when his girlfriend's co-workers formed a circle around him and verbally blasted him for treating their friend badly. And since he rode to the park on the company's bus, he was stuck for the entire day. Not only did David end up walking around the park alone, he became doubly embarrassed when it came time to board the bus and return home because by then everyone knew about the earlier incident and chatted openly about it with one another. He arrived home that night with a very bad headache, finally willing to take responsibility for what happened to him that day. This experience served as the catalyst for David to change how he treated women. A couple of years later, he met someone who enjoyed the same things and they have been married for close to 10 years. David's commitment to breaking the pattern of treating women badly was the underlying structure for recognizing his own fear of choosing the wrong mate.

David's actions are a good example of how many people tend to repeat past mistakes until an event occurs that causes us to examine our behavior. Both men and women make many relationship mistakes that cause each other a great deal of pain and anguish. Many of the men I talk to face the same challenges of my female clients who are nursing the wounds of a love relationship that has gone wrong, sometimes for many years afterwards. The difference is women will openly discuss their emotional issues with one another, while men keep their feelings locked up and will not admit their hurts because they do not want to appear weak. The inability of men to talk openly is one of the factors that plays a role in whether they are able to achieve their dreams, hopes and desires.

The biggest factor I have found, which often blocks both men and women from finding the right love formula, is that once they are in a good relationship, they tend to stop the same honest conversations they had with their mate when they first started dating.

My discussion with my male clients makes me feel hopeful that most of them recognize their communication challenges and they are working long and hard to "talk out loud" about their concerns. The key to being an evolved male in today's world is to truthfully discuss what is going on, and when a problem develops, seek the counsel of a trusted professional. A good plan for any guy who wants to be pro-active in his growth and development is to schedule twice-yearly appointments with a person they trust and respect to discuss their future life plan. The hardest part for most men is being open to getting help. Whenever there are fires brewing on any front—professionally or personally—the time to talk about them is before they erupt into a bonfire.

Here are the tips evolved males need to follow to stay healthy:

1. Find a person who they feel safe to discuss their thoughts and feelings without being concerned with being perceived as being weak.
2. Go to the doctor for regular health exams and discuss their problems with the people who mean the most to them.
3. Do not make finances the primary consideration in decisions that are made.
4. Make the time and commitment to attend male-only support groups.

Our dreams serve as a wonderful connective force that reunites us with those we have loved and lost. The lessons revealed in these night visions provide us with the guidance and direction needed to move forward in our lives. Keeping a dream journal is one of the best things you can do to capture and reinforce the inner wisdom revealed to you.

One of my most vivid dreams involved my grandmother, Edna Mae Terrell. One of the things I missed most when she died was the wonderful aroma from the meals she prepared in her kitchen. In addition to the spicy New Orleans-style red beans and rice she often fixed, my grandmother also served a big dish of kick-ass whenever she felt someone needed to be told off.

This particular dream occurred on December 10, 1999. I know the exact date because it moved me so deeply that I got up at 2:30 in the morning and recorded the whole thing in my journal.

The dream started with me walking down the streets of New Orleans when a friend told me that I had to sample the food at a new restaurant. Suddenly, I found myself inside a bustling establishment, and the friend who took me there insisted that we had to go into the kitchen to meet the cook. It was none other than Grandma Edna Mae. She was looking so good and putting out slamming meals. I felt a deep pull in my heart seeing her like that. The last time I had seen my grandmother, her frail 97-year-old body was at the end of her life's journey. What a joy it was to be in her presence again!

Ever since I was in my teens, my grandparents lived on the second floor of my parents' three-flat building on Chicago's south side. It was commonplace on Sundays for their apartment to be filled with family. And of course, you could always find Grandma cooking in her kitchen, the same way I saw her in my dream. Being there with her even for those few minutes made me feel like I had a warm blanket of love wrapped all around me.

As I hugged her in my dream, Grandma told me, "Look around closely, Sheree. Things are changing very quickly."

My mind tried to wrap itself around the significance of her words, but every sense of my being was connected with seeing my grandmother once again. The next thing I knew, I was sitting on the side of my bed, feeling both glad and sad to have spent time with her, only then to realize she was gone again.

After writing down the dream, I waited three-and-a-half hours before calling my mother promptly at 6 a.m. to tell her about it. When I finished describing the dream to Mom, I heard myself say, "I wonder who she is coming to get?"

Mom immediately questioned why I felt that way, but there were no rational words to explain what I just said to her. Our conversation ended and I released the dream just like you would a good cup of tea when it started to get cold.

This particular day, my to-do list was filled to capacity, as my husband and I were two days away from hosting a holiday champagne party in our home for 50 friends and relatives.

My mind swirled with everything from handling a sales call for my business to picking up a clothing rack to buying another case of champagne. As I pulled into the driveway of my office, it hit me that I had not seen my parents all week.

Coming into my office, I told my assistant, Julia Turner, the necessary details of my successful sales call and the work that needed to be done for our client. Suddenly, my mind returned to my not having seen my parents. Julia tried to convince me that my already packed schedule was too tight to finish all the things that needed to be done, and she reminded me that they would be at the party in a couple of days.

The inner nudge I felt was too strong to ignore, so I decided to forgo writing up the sales order and drove my car over the three blocks to where my parents lived.

I smiled when getting out of the car, recalling all the times Mom and Dad had always been there for my daughter and me.

Almost from the moment my daughter was born, my mom would show up at my doorstep telling me that she simply had to see her grandchild. Once Brittany started to talk, it was not unusual to hear her call out "Grandmommy," and then a few minutes later my doorbell would ring and Mom would be there. The connection that existed between them was uncanny. Dad was equally important in my daughter's life. He stepped up and became more than a grandfather, filling in on everything from picking her up at school to soothing her tears when her feelings were hurt over her father's absence.

When I walked into my parents' home, Dad was seated on the living room couch watching The Jerry Springer Show. As usual, the program had some crazy people going off on each other. Seeing this, I shook my head and laughed and grabbed my father's hand, telling him to get up and come with me to the liquor store to purchase another case of champagne for Sunday's party.

My parents' apartment was more crowded than usual that day due to a surprise visit from my brother Eric and his wife Angela with their two young children. My oldest brother Horace also lived with my parents, and he was helping Mom dish out food for everyone. While seeing them gathered in the living room for a moment, my mind flashed back to my dream as my mom looked at me. Although I did not mention our earlier talk again, I wondered if my mother was also thinking about it now, as we were seated across the table from one another. Was it my imagination or did I suddenly feel my grandmother's presence in the room with us? I did not know, but I remained silent on the matter.

After finishing our meal, my father and I left to go to a liquor store just under a mile away. We chatted about the upcoming party and some of my business concerns.

Once we reached the store, I took the cart and pushed while my father debated the prices of champagne. Dad was a retired grocery store owner and still took great pride in being able to calculate the best value for your dollar. He easily figured out the amount of champagne we needed for the party and announced, "We already have enough, but it would be wise to buy one more case, just to be sure."

A store clerk came up, took our request, and sent us to the front of the store to pay for our purchase. We declined the clerk's offer to take the case of champagne to my car, knowing that it would not be a problem for my father to put it in the trunk. When he lifted it up, I heard him make a slight grunt. For a moment, I wondered if the box was too heavy, but I dismissed the thought since all my life my strong father had always been able to handle everything without a problem.

We were quickly on our way back to my parents' house without me giving a second thought to the slight nagging feeling inside of me. I dropped off my father and told him we were looking forward to seeing him and Mom at the party.

Four short hours later, the phone rang and Jim, my husband, answered it. He had a strange look on his face when he handed me the phone after talking for a few minutes. "It's your mother," he said. My mom could be a notorious practical joker and I wondered if she told my husband her favorite line: "Women's faults are many. Men have only two—everything they say and everything they do."

I felt a little uneasy taking the phone and continued to push forward in the same fast mode I had been operating in all day. I wanted mom to tell me quickly why she called so I could finally take my clothes off and relax. Upon hearing the sound of her voice, I knew something was very wrong. She began simply, "Sheree, I've got bad news."

There were a number of people in our family who were not doing well at the time, and my mind quickly assembled a list. Mom quickly replied "no" to each name I called. Finally, I asked her point blank who the phone call was about. "It's your father."

That was enough to send my mind into a complete state of shock, and the next thing I knew my knees buckled, leaving me on the floor in my bedroom as my mind tried to process my mother's words.

"What's wrong with Dad?" I screamed loudly. "I was there less than four hours ago. What could have happened in such a short time?"

Mom explained to me how dad went out to the front of the house to warm up the car, as he usually did, for them to go visit my Aunt Rae in a nearby nursing home.

When my mother reached for the passenger door and found it locked, she immediately thought my father was playing one of his practical jokes. She was sure of it when walking around to the other side of the car, finding him with his head down, looking like he was pretending to be asleep. But her husband of 50 years did not respond, no matter how many times she knocked on the window to tell him to open up the door and stop playing.

Mom's internal alarm kicked in right away, and she ran back to the building to get the extra car keys and my two brothers.

They quickly got the door open and placed my father on the ground right by the car, starting CPR. They called 911 and an ambulance responded in less than five minutes. My father was taken to a nearby hospital.

My sense is that my father died in his car, in front of the house, just moments before he was going to be driving in rush-hour traffic. My heart pounded in my chest as I tried to process what happened and

told me the innermost details of his passing. He said that it was the hardest thing for Mom to come and find him in the car like that. "I would have given anything for her not to have to go through that." And then he revealed something so keenly insightful that it connected all the dots in the universe for me. "It was the easiest thing. One minute I was there, and the next minute your grandmother was serving me a meal."

I think about Dad all the time and remember that night when he taught me in my dream that everything in life is connected. To this day, I still make it a habit of recording my dreams.

Keeping a dream journal is an excellent tool to help you in sharpening your intuitive muscle. The information you receive when your brain is relaxed operates at a deeper level of consciousness and many times will reveal things you might not consider when you are awake.

Here are the steps for keeping a dream journal:

1. Find a notebook or journal specifically to record your dreams. Keep it within arm's reach of the bed. Dreams fade quickly upon awakening, so you need to write them down as soon as you wake up.

2. Note the time and date of your dream. Then write down everything you can remember. Try to recall everything from the time of the day to the color of the room and even what people are wearing.

3. Identify dream themes. Think about the location, sounds, sensations, colors, objects, people and the emotions you feel in the dream.

4. Do not worry about spelling or grammar. As long as you can

read your own writing, you can decipher it later.

5. If you can, draw or sketch any images from the dream. You do not have to be an artist to visualize what went on during your dream.

6. Jot down any major life issues that you are going through at the time of the dream. Everything is connected to everything else. Over time, you will be able to link your subconscious dream to things going on in your real life.

7. Give the dream an appropriate title. It does not have to be anything fancy. In fact, less is more when it comes to naming a dream.

None of us knows when we will be called to serve during the journey of life. That was clearly the case with me when it came to providing for the care of my 55-year-old mentally challenged male cousin, Kevin.

My life took a dramatic change when I decided to follow my intuition and do a wellness check on my cousin, Kevin, and his father, my Uncle Jones. It was not like I acted on my feelings right away. It took me a couple of months before I gave in to the gentle nudges that awakened me each morning urging me to go see them. Finally, one morning the nudges turned into a loud message that I could no longer ignore. I tried to bargain with myself by agreeing to do it one day sometime soon, but after making that deal, a sickening feeling in my stomach made me decide it had to be done immediately.

Before my dad's death, he was the one who checked on his brother's family. It was not easy dealing with them. My 84-year-old Uncle Jones drank too much and Kevin could be moody and temperamental on his good days.

Life was not always like that for them. My Uncle Jones had been a decorated Army veteran in World War II. He worked and retired from a job as a Pullman porter. This was considered an esteemed profession for Negro men during that time, but it meant he spent a lot of time away from home, working long hours for low wages.

Uncle Jones was handsome with dark wavy hair and a light-brown complexion that turned red when he drank. He married my Aunt Eula late in life. She was 46 years old when Kevin was born. The family noticed that their son always had a vacant look in his eyes and cried a lot. Everyone suspected that something was wrong with him, but in the 1950s, people did not talk about learning disabilities or mental challenges like they do today.

Uncle Jones, Aunt Eula and Kevin lived in a large apartment on the south side of Chicago in Woodlawn, a neighborhood once considered fashionable. Today, it is the kind of area where you want to arrive early and leave well before dark. After Aunt Eula's death over 20 years ago, we saw less and less of Uncle Jones and Kevin at family gatherings.

It felt like time was frozen in their large, spacious apartment, with my aunt's funeral program sitting on the small table in the living room along with piles of old newspapers and magazines stacked high.

During an earlier visit, I asked Uncle Jones if he was open to bringing in help to clean their apartment. His response was to turn up the volume on the baseball game on the large television that sat in the middle of everything.

The day of my visit, Chicago was in the midst of a heat wave very similar to the one in 1995 when over 100 people died. Many of those who perished faced the same challenges that my uncle and cousin did—they were isolated senior citizens suffering from mental problems and living in out-of-control home environments. Experts say even the simplest cases require family and professional assistance.

Sitting in my car in front of their building that day, I struggled with myself over having to go inside and asked out loud, "Why me?" When no one answered, I realized there were no other options but to finally go in.

Things felt strange from the moment after I rang the bell on the outside gate, when I was quickly buzzed in without my uncle or cousin asking me to identify myself like they normally do. It was 85 degrees outside, but it felt a lot hotter when I walked into the hallway of their building. Climbing up three flights of stairs did not help matters any, and I felt perspiration trickle down my back. On the way up, I started to bargain with myself. "Sheree, you only have to stay for 20 or 30 minutes."

It was Kevin who answered the door when I knocked. He was dressed only in pajama bottoms, and his bare chest was dripping with perspiration. My cousin is a big guy, nearly six feet tall, with a light complexion and curly black hair. What distinguishes Kevin is the ever-present blank look in his eyes, a large head, and legs and feet that appear swollen.

"My God, it must be over 100 degrees in here," I said, walking through the doorway.

Kevin seemed unfazed by my comment as he waddled back to resume watching a soap opera on a small black and white television that sat perched on the dresser in the back bedroom off the kitchen. Taking a look around, everything felt "off." The front of the apartment was totally dark, and it was so hot. My mind tried to process what to do, and I figured the first thing was to check on my uncle. Questioning my cousin about his whereabouts only produced a grunt and a wave towards the front of the apartment.

Every nerve in my body was on edge as I walked down the long hallway. A muffled sound appeared to be coming from the bedroom to my right. As I slowly glanced in the room, my worst fears materialized. When he saw me, Uncle Jones struggled to sit up from beneath the thin, dirty sheet that covered him. His efforts to talk were limited to unintelligible mumbling. I realized that something had to be done quickly and I raced back to the kitchen in search of ice and water. I heard myself scream when a mouse darted in front of me. Grabbing some ice from the refrigerator, a large pitcher of water and a towel, I ran back to my uncle's room. After a few sips of water and icing his brow, I realized that my uncle and his son needed urgent care. I pulled my cell phone out of my pocket and called 911.

My voice quivered as I described the situation to the kind operator. She asked me questions while telling me that paramedics were on their way. The five to eight minutes it took for them to arrive felt like the longest moments I have ever experienced in my life.

While waiting, I prayed for my uncle and cousin, for myself and especially for the paramedics who came running through the door. They ran up three flights of stairs in that extreme heat and started helping immediately. To this day, I still think of them as God's angels. The paramedics examined my Uncle Jones first. They diagnosed him as being severely dehydrated with highly elevated blood pressure and an irregular heartbeat. Next, they questioned my cousin and found out both of them had not taken their medications in over two weeks. They were both taken to the hospital for further assessment.

The next day, representatives from the departments of aging and human services met with me to explain how things had to change if Kevin and his father were to remain in their apartment. Because the situation was rated a "crisis," a nurse was assigned to come in three times a week to assess their status. In the meantime, I was given one week to clean up the apartment or Kevin and Uncle Jones would be forced to relocate to a nursing home.

I hired a team of three men and, together, we were able to clean up the place enough for them to return home. The City of Chicago was called regarding problems with my Uncle's apartment, and the initially reluctant landlord immediately arranged to fix the wiring that had caused the fuse to blow whenever my uncle and cousin attempted to run their air conditioner.

There were times I felt like I was going crazy overextending myself. One day Kevin screamed and yelled at me so much that I knew how people felt who had high blood pressure. He got upset after listening to representatives from the different agencies telling us what we had to do in order to keep them at home. While I understood he was frightened, there were times when I wanted to walk away.

My strongest influence in continuing to assist them was my dad. Even though he was no longer alive, I knew what he would have expected of me. Two of my siblings—my sister Juanita and my brother Horace—also assisted in every way they could. For nearly three months, we took on the massive job of cleaning out 30 years of clutter from Uncle Jones and Kevin's apartment. It was not pretty or easy. Sometimes, after being at their place, I woke up at night feeling like bugs were crawling on me.

One of my most memorable experiences in helping them to clean their place happened when we found my uncle's old army uniform in the closet. Somehow in the midst of all the clutter, the uniform had been preserved in a suit bag. When I pulled it out, it took me a moment to process what I had in my hands - a family treasure. I called my Uncle Jones in, and when he saw the uniform he broke out into a smile. The man who had worn this soldier's garment was now hidden in the frail body standing on a cane. Suddenly my intuition took over and I asked, "Do you want to try it on?" He shrugged slightly at first as if it did not matter, but I sensed that my uncle did want to put on the jacket. Placing his cane against the wall, I decided to just help him into the uniform. I wish you could have been there for that moment...it was so precious. One of my deepest regrets is that I did not have a camera to record this special moment. My father's brother stood up straighter as he looked at himself in the mirror. He even saluted himself. This rare glimpse into the heart of the man I had not really known before would never have happened until my intuition intervened.

Uncle Jones passed away about six months after Horace, Juanita and I became more involved in his life. Afterwards, we were faced with the dilemma of what would happen with Kevin. We visited various agencies that worked with providing housing for special needs adults.

This was the time when I fully surrendered myself over to prayer. There was so much to do and the allotted time for moving Kevin out of the apartment was quickly drawing to a close. I believe that divine intervention played an important role in having everything that we needed coming together. My husband had a business friend who owned a senior building and was able to place Kevin in an apartment just a couple of weeks before he had to vacate the other premises.

A high school friend, Wanda Lenoir, referred me to an organization to get the necessary testing to determine my cousin's mental status. Kevin was diagnosed as mildly retarded with the decision-making ability of a 12-year-old. Armed with the diagnosis, he became eligible to live in government-assisted housing.

For two years, Juanita, Horace and I became a unified team. We took Kevin into our hearts, accompanying him to his doctor appointments and helping with grocery shopping while especially making sure he cleaned his apartment.

Being involved with a special needs person has taught me greater tolerance, understanding and compassion. It also helped me grow in my work as a counselor and coach, and I have learned to even more strongly trust my intuition. What I learned, without a doubt, is that the call to serve does not come in the package you expect, and that many times we ignore the call for service because it is not convenient or, in my uncle's and cousin's cases, it is too messy.

There were numerous miracles that happened to my family when we got involved with caring for Kevin. He no longer spends his time watching soap operas and eating all day. My cousin initially attended an adult program at Leeda Services of Illinois.* The staff was extremely kind and caring and even provided services for Kevin when the state lagged behind on funding.

Eventually, Kevin was approved for state funding and has moved into an apartment setting with three other at-risk male adults. He spends

*A portion of the sale of this book will be donated to Leeda Services of Illinois.

his time now working at the office of Leeda Services of Illinois and lives in a community where he is safe and protected. In addition, Kevin is studying to take his General Educational Development (GED) exam.

I do not want to think about what would have happened if I had not listened to my intuition and responded by checking on my uncle and cousin. That is the thing about when we are called to give service — you never know when it will occur. Giving at that level was new for me, and there were many times when I wanted to walk away. It indeed might come down to the question of "Why me?" The answer can very well be revealed in the heart and mind of the person whose face you see in the mirror.

Here are tips to help you navigate your intuition to assist your family and friends:

1. Check regularly in on your elderly family, neighbors and friends; this is part of being a good human being.

2. Make a list of resources to turn to for assistance in caring for the elderly, including aarp.org and various city, county and state agencies, as well as friends and family.

3. Be in a peaceful state when you interact with seniors.

4. Remember that everyone gets old and one day you will need help.

5. Say "God help me," when you do not know what to do during a difficult situation.

6. Take deep breaths to help you decide if you need to call 911 during emergency situations.

Have you ever gotten so angry that your wrath almost triggered a violent argument? I experienced this level of rage during a chance encounter with a woman on the street, and it served as a major wake-up call to the danger of allowing my emotions to get out of control. Getting into a bitter quarrel with a stranger is one decision that I will always regret, but it also served as one of the most powerful learning experiences in my life.

My husband and I were walking to lunch in our neighborhood one weekday afternoon after we shopped for furniture for our outdoor terrace. Like many couples, we had spent more money than we planned, and as we walked, we quarreled over whose fault it was that we exceeded our budget. In a matter of minutes, a casual stroll turned into a full-fledged argument. Our raised voices attracted the attention of a woman who was walking a small poodle near us. Lost in the moment, I suddenly realized that the dog was barking in circles around my feet. Trying to process everything that was going on, I said to no one in particular, "What the hell is this dog doing here?"

The woman gave me a piercing look and her words hit me like a sharp punch when she said, "He is barking, like you are."

I wish I could tell you that I turned the other cheek and ignored her remark. Instead, we entered into a volley of yelling, screaming and cursing at each other like two crazy people. I can still remember the tightness in my stomach as the anger raged out-of-control in my body. Logic and common sense were ripped from my mind as I allowed my temper to flare to the point where I connected to the same emotional turmoil many of us experienced as small children.

The woman who hurled insults at me did not look menacing. She was about my height with long blonde hair, and we were both dressed in the same casual summer clothing. The only visible difference between us was that she was white and my husband and I are both black. The amazing part in that whole insane, out-of-control drama was that neither of us made any racial attacks on the other. We were just two angry women caught in a web of hostility that spiraled out of control.

For some reason, in this crazy cosmic world, our accidental meeting opened the doorway to an emotional tsunami. And there is no doubt in my mind that the small poodle with its irritating bark only became menacing due to the loud voices coming from my husband and me.

I vaguely remember seeing people walk by, staring at the woman and me as we flung insults at each other. They probably thought we had a long held resentment or grudge against the other, rather than two total strangers who met at the wrong time and place.

My husband tried to intervene by explaining to the woman that our conversation was a private matter and not directed at her. This only seemed to inflame her more, because next she waved her finger in my face, telling me to shut up. At that point, I actually started to see the color red. I could sense my brain slowing down, and I visualized red covering everything from the cars passing by on the street to the woman standing in front of me yelling. Even now, while recalling this incident, I am shaking my head in disbelief wondering how a bitter argument with a woman I did not even know could escalate so quickly to the point where I lost control.

The price we pay in losing ourselves is more important than many of us realize. My body shook with rage as I told my husband to step out of the way, readying myself to fight a complete stranger.

Suddenly, right before violence could explode between the two of us, I began to observe my actions like a slow-motion movie. I saw what I believed could be the potential outcome of a physical encounter, with an image in my mind of the woman lying on the ground. I believe in that moment, the power of grace flooded in and transformed the surrounding energy before violence erupted to the point where one of us would have hurt the other or been arrested.

None of us leaves home planning on getting into an argument like this. We live our lives operating within our own internal database filled with our own set of resentments, hurts and anger. Our system crashes when an incident takes us over the edge.

Once clarity flooded into my mind, I realized the danger of allowing things to continue. My attempt to apologize to the very angry woman fell on deaf ears, as she was not ready or willing to disconnect from the emotional thunderstorm going on inside of her. It was very hard for me to release my own feelings, but after having a glimpse of the possible outcome of this argument, I knew the only thing to do was stop before something bad happened.

At that point, I started to back away, clearly seeing the shock in the stranger's eyes as she continued to barrage me with names and obscenities. Very slowly, my husband took my arm, and I started walking in the direction of the restaurant where we were originally headed. While we walked, I focused on feeling love in my heart, and finally the pounding in my chest started to subside. It was a bad decision for me to allow my anger to reach a point of uncontrollable rage, and I did not intend to give away my power again. We eventually lost track of how long it took for the woman to stop following us. At some point, we noticed that she and the barking dog were gone. I stumbled that day big time on the test of controlling my emotions. The indescribable, uncontrollable rage I experienced was so overwhelming that it changed me. Whenever there is a risk that I could get into a heated argument, I make a decision to either end the conversation or completely remove myself from the situation. I have even cautiously intervened when other people are at the point of losing control and quietly suggested to others to walk away before something bad happens. One man thanked me afterwards and asked me why I stopped to intervene. I told him, "I have walked in your shoes."

My husband and I ate a quiet lunch that day. I prayed for the woman I encountered to have peace, also asking her forgiveness for my anger flaring to the point where it almost led to violence.

Going through this experience taught me to approach life like a chess game, to play each step carefully and consciously before making a move. I may never completely vanquish anger from my life experience, but I can definitely control how much it affects me and how I react to others. What I have learned is that I must be aware of the internal warning signs that are present inside of me. Seeing red is what alerted me to the extreme danger of violence occurring. The tightness in my stomach was another indicator that my decision to continue arguing was not a wise one.

None of us knows when something will happen that will cause us to be upset to the point of losing control. There's so much stress and tension in many of our lives that we do not know our emotions have reached a boiling point until we explode.

Before this incident happened, if I were asked to take a survey questioning whether I was capable of a violent outburst, my answer would have been resoundingly, "No." Yet realizing my limitations is critical to how I approach and live my life going forward.

Many of us think we know what we would do in an extreme situation. In random encounters, it is hard to take a step back and consider what the other person might be going through. We all have issues and challenges, and when we become ensnarled in emotional turmoil, it is hard to be rational and objective. Each of us has the powerful ability to observe ourselves and assess consciously when we must correct or adjust our thoughts, feelings and actions before something awful happens.

To recap, here are the steps on how to recognize and change negative emotional patterns in your life:

1. Pay attention to what's going on inside your body and immediately notice whenever your emotions are out of control.

2. Ask people you trust and respect if you have a negative emotional pattern that needs to be watched.

3. Recognize the people and circumstances that cause your emotions to reach a boiling point. Once you do, determine the best course of action to take whenever this pattern emerges in your life.

4. Embrace the God-given power of free will and choose to let things go.

5. Keep your body healthy by not allowing the emotions of hate, anger, resentment, fear and guilt to disrupt the natural balance in your life.

Trusting is the biggest challenge when it comes to acting on the information we receive from our intuition. This is because many of us are not comfortable in dealing with the emotion of fear. When we feel afraid, our mental clarity goes out the window and we often ignore what is right in front of us.

Each of us needs to think intuitively, especially when it comes to our personal safety. We encounter all kinds of people each day, and there are always good and bad folks around us. We often cannot afford to give someone the benefit of the doubt; this is why connecting with your intuition is so important, as it will help you to determine who to trust and who to keep at arm's length. Ignoring our inner wisdom can lead us to become victims of crime, violence and even death.

In a harrowing example, my friend Jewel was parking one afternoon after grocery shopping when she noticed a teenager across the street watching an older man walking on a cane. In only a few seconds, she immediately sensed danger, so she opened her car window and spoke to the senior citizen while he walked. Feeling that her presence let the teenager know someone was watching, Jewel relaxed and enjoyed a brief conversation with the man. After the elderly man continued his walk down the block, she got out of her car. Having dismissed the earlier warning sign, she walked to the rear of her vehicle and opened her trunk only to have the teenager suddenly reappear, pointing an automatic weapon at Jewel's forehead and demanding her purse.

Jewel's purse was stolen that day. Luckily, the robber let her go without hurting her. Later, as she recalled the incident, my friend said the biggest lesson she learned was to continue to remain aware from the moment your inner wisdom first senses there is danger until you know for sure that you are safe.

News reports every day are filled with similar stories of what happened to Jewel. Violence has become all too commonplace in America. National security expert Gavin de Becker, author of *The Gift of Fear*, says the gift of your internal guardian stands ready to warn you of hazards and to guide you through risky situations.

De Becker warns in his book that strangers are often not the only people who are most likely to hurt us. He says women in particular often face danger from their husbands or boyfriends. The author stresses the best way for women to avoid becoming a victim is to listen to their intuition and to take immediate action when it comes to the people we allow into our lives.

The main reason many of us do not consciously choose to connect with our intuition is that our Western society does not encourage the use of it. We rely on technology much more than we do our instincts. De Becker calls intuition our most complex cognitive process and, at the same time, the simplest one to use.

When you learn how to feel peaceful inside yourself and not allow your mind to be constantly bombarded with problems and worries, you are more likely to notice when something feels wrong.

Being aware of your intuition requires that you understand the thin line between worry and fear. Worry is voluntary; it is something we choose to do. Many of us do not realize we have developed the habit of worrying all the time.

Once you have lived long enough and made enough mistakes, you will realize how much unnecessary stress we bring to our lives by worrying. Monitoring your self-talk is the best way to determine if worrying has become a constant habit in your life.

When we release the tendency to constantly worry, this actually frees our minds to become more aware of our intuition. Feelings of anxiety or focusing on everything that can go wrong actually prevents us from paying attention to the subtle signs and clues that are always accessible. Once you have learned to be consciously aware of your thoughts, we can easily sharpen our intuitive muscles by developing the habit of people watching.

Begin by developing the habit of observing people who are near or around you at all times. Training yourself to stay alert will help you to connect with your inner wisdom. It will also act as an internal radar and quickly help you assess if you are at risk.

Developing the habit of checking in with my intuition has repeatedly kept me out of harm's way. One summer afternoon, as I was leaving my office in downtown Chicago, I quickly scanned all four directions around me. As I turned to my left, there was a young man walking down the block heading east. He was holding his neck and wearing what appeared to be a white t-shirt covered completely in blood. The moment felt so surreal that I experienced what many call déjà vu, feeling that this scene was from a movie. I followed my intuition, called 911, and described the young man to an operator who said, "The police know about the attack."

When I questioned why I did not hear a police or ambulance siren attending to the young man, she said, "The police cannot be everywhere at the same time," and that there was an attack going on near where I was located.

My hair stood up on the back of my neck as I began to quickly plan how to quickly leave the area. Instead of waiting for the bus as I planned, I started walking south and crossed a busy intersection, where I encountered another young man on the corner talking on his cell phone. Since we were only a foot apart from each other, I kept my eyes on him even as my feet were moving. Not only did I continue to maintain visual contact with the man, but I also focused all my concentration inward to the point where I began to feel like everything was slowing down around me.

My efforts to stay tuned in paid off as I heard the young man say to whomever he was talking to on his cell phone, "I am going to let this one go." I felt that hearing his words was an omen and I commanded my intuition to stay alert as I pulled my purse closer to my side. I also grabbed my keys in my pocket and held them between my fingers in order to strike someone in the eye if they attempted to attack me. My actions were part dictated by what I read in the book *Survive the Unthinkable: A Total Guide to Women's Self-Protection* by Tim Larkin. In less than a moment, I quickly made the decision to injure anyone who tried to attack me.

Most of us have a natural disinclination towards violence, but that day I turned my inner signal on and willfully set the intention to claw at the eyes of anyone who came up and tried to hurt me. My body, mind and spirit were engaged in only what can be described as fighter mode, and I believe my will to survive was so strong the young man on the phone knew intuitively that I would not give up without a brutal fight. There is no one formula on how to survive a violent attack. Our best defense is to stay focused and aware at all times so, if we find our safety at risk, we can do everything possible to keep ourselves safe. Learning how to use your intuition when it comes to your personal safety is a valuable tool everyone should learn and use on a daily basis.

As we age, the ability to access our intuition has the power to expand our consciousness and to adjust for the changes that are always going on around us. While we may not be able to run as fast as or have greater strength than a person who attempts to attack us, a sharp mind can quickly assess danger and direct us to take action rather than sit around and wait to see what will happen. Our body is our best teacher for being aware of our inner knowledge. Our internal laboratory is always giving us clues to what is going on around us. Intuition is not passive; it is an active energy, which affects everything we do.

Recognizing the signs of déjà vu is what alerted me to the risk of danger that day. Whenever I have a strong sensation that an event or experience or a person reminds me of something from the past, I feel the hair on my neck stand up.

Learning your own internal signs of intuition is critical. Develop the habit of setting the intention to connect with your inner wisdom every day when you first wake up. Also, visualize a beautiful shield of protective light surrounding you, your communities and your families. Before you enter your home and/or any new environment, develop the habit of allowing yourself to "feel" what is going on before you go inside. Always do a quick check-in before getting into an elevator or other confined spaces. Do not be concerned about hurting someone's feelings if you decide not to enter somewhere you don't feel safe.

Recently, I went to see a female podiatrist whose office was located in a large commercial building that did not have an intercom system or a front desk with a security person. I felt uneasy and decided to keep my antenna up while walking to the second floor of the doctor's office. Even though the podiatrist came highly recommended, her personal safety habits left a lot to be desired. There was no doorbell or buzz-in system to prevent anyone from entering her office, and the physician lazily left her purse in the small, empty reception area that opened to a long, dimly lit hallway. I discussed with her the lack of security and the fact that her purse was left unattended.

Even though she provided excellent service, I would not use her again or recommend her to my network. Her safety habits left me feeling vulnerable, and even while she worked on me in her office I kept my antenna up to be aware if someone entered the small reception area with the unattended purse.

Staying alert and aware of our senses plays an important factor in keeping us safe. Let's face it: The potential to become a victim is greater when we are either mindlessly talking on our cell phone or not paying attention to what is going on around us in some other way.

Also, in my sessions with both my male and female clients, I have noticed most people are more likely to ignore their intuitive hunches when it involves a person they are romantically involved with.

Take my client "Maria," a 28-year-old IT specialist who chose not to pay attention to her inner wisdom when she too got involved with a man who was in the dangerous profession of being a loan shark. When her new boyfriend showered her with new clothes, a car and furniture, Maria pushed aside the nagging voice in her head that told her not to accept the gifts. Instead, she decided to take all the presents her new boyfriend offered. After giving away her old things, she began feeling very stylish, and Maria began to think of herself as having risen to a level above her family and friends. But the pretty clothes and new car did not blind Maria's friends from commenting on how jumpy she now seemed since she started dating the new man. When she came to see me as a client, the IT specialist told me that her friends were jealous of her new man and wealth.

The 28-year-old made an appointment with me after having a recurring dream of being lost in a maze. My sense was that the dream symbolized Maria "being lost" due to the bad decisions she was making in her life. I never believed that the executive secretary's friends and family were envious of her new fur coat or BMW; rather, they noticed she became nervous at having to be at a particular place and time whenever her boyfriend called. Choosing to be with the loan shark meant Maria was no longer in charge of her life because her boyfriend expected her to be home even if he did not come over. During the rare times when the two of them did go out on a date, he spent most of the time talking in low tones on his cell phone. When Maria decided to end the relationship, her boyfriend immediately demanded all his gifts be returned. It was a very difficult lesson for my client to learn that you cannot get something for nothing. At one point, various male family members moved in with her to ensure her safety. She is now in the process of rebuilding her life.

It is easy for anyone to become blinded by material trappings such as fancy cars and expensive gifts, making us prone to ignore the serious questions we should ask about the people we bring into our lives. This also happened to "Janice," a 38-year-old retail makeup specialist, when she started dating a man who always had lots of money. She told me, "Intuitively, I knew the money did not come from a regular job." Janice was right. She found out two months into the relationship that "John," 43, laundered money for a living. The couple had been together for over a year when they married and purchased their first home. Once they moved in, it was commonplace for material items in the home to appear and disappear without explanation. One day the makeup specialist had a panic attack at work and was astute enough to realize that her anxiety was based on what her husband did for a living. The two finally had a frank conversation about the toll her husband's work was having on her health. Hoping to salvage the relationship, her husband supported Janice in pursuing her long-time dream of becoming a teacher.

Janice diligently applied herself and earned a bachelor's and master's degree in education. Eventually, she faced the reality that her husband's profession conflicted with her personal values. After graduating from school, Janice transitioned into a teaching career. While she is highly respected in her field, this experienced educator is rightfully concerned about not repeating her pattern of "being attracted to bad boys." As a result, she has not pursued a serious relationship since her marriage ended two years ago.

Pursing her dream to become a teacher was the catalyst for Janice to rewrite the script for changing a destructive pattern that existed in her marriage. Focusing her attention on a positive goal gave her the confidence and strength to finally end her marriage. Men and women who want to triumph in love must use all of their talents, skills and abilities to make better choices in the people they choose to love. None of us can allow ourselves to be swept away with emotion and ignore the vital warning signs that are always available to us through our inner wisdom.

The way to change the dating game whenever we meet someone who we think could be a good mate is to ask your intuition to reveal to you:

Does this person mean me harm or good?

Each of us must enhance and expand our selection process or we will most likely continue the pattern of poor relationship choices. It is interesting to note, I have seen many female clients who have chosen to be in relationships and even marry "bad boys." I have not seen one male client who has made the same mistake.

What makes it even more difficult for people to make good relationship choices is the fact that a record number of people are turning to dating sites to find a mate. Currently, there are 41 million people who are looking for love on the Internet. I am amazed at the number of smart people who go on a dating site and immediately trust the person who emailed and text messaged them without any questions. The people you meet on dating sites are strangers and should be treated as such.

Whenever a client comes in and tells me about the wonderful person they met online, I remind them of the sage wisdom of "buyer beware." If a person sounds too good to be true, usually, he or she is. I always suggest a professional background check to ensure that the person we think we know is who he or she is in real life. Yes, I do believe in love, but I also am a strong advocate of common sense.

One of the most memorable quotes by Maya Angelou, provides valuable insight that everyone should practice, "When someone shows you who they are believe them; the first time."

Anyone who is considering a new dating companion should listen very closely to Angelou's sage wisdom. All too often, the relationship mistakes we make put not only our own lives at risk but also our children's. If you use online dating, make safety a top priority.

In my work, I have noticed women and men tend to be most vulnerable after they have been "burned" in a bad relationship. The best way to ensure that your next relationship does not repeat the same pattern is by examining the warning signs we previously ignored. People come to us with clues all the time, and it is only when we consciously choose to pay closer attention that we will know who to let go of and who to accept into our lives. The information is always there if we choose to listen.

It is all too common for my clients to admit that they completely overlooked the danger signs in a potential mate until it was too late. If you do not trust yourself and your own intuition to alert you when something does not feel right about a person, ask a trusted friend or confidant to tell you their impression of the individual. And if this friend confirms that there is a potential risk from the dating partner you are involved with, walk away early rather than waiting until they have stolen your identity or valued possessions, or maybe even physically hurt you.

Rushing into intimacy is one of the main reasons our intuition gets pushed aside. Your best bet for remaining safe is to cautiously enter into a relationship with anyone you meet online. Research shows that people who meet on the Internet enter into an intimate relationship on the first or second date. Once they become emotionally involved, it is not unusual for couples to exchange keys to each other's homes between the twelfth and fourteenth dates. Because our society's values have shifted regarding women taking the initiative sexually, there is a greater incidence of females making the first step to become intimate with a man they meet online. In a 2010 survey, just over one third of the women who date online say they "would make the first move." If you date online, there's a high chance you will break up online within five to eight months of meeting. According to Match.com, 48% of their singles break up via email.

Take the time to get to know a person before allowing them into your bed. In Steve Harvey's book *Act Like A Lady, Think Like A Man*, he suggests a woman hold off on sexual intimacy with a man until they pass the 90-day test. I think Harvey's advice is good for men also. In addition to heeding his advice, do the most thorough background check you can afford at the very beginning. Taking the time to test the relationship before things get hot and heavy will prevent you from making careless mistakes when you cannot think straight.

Take my client "Melody," 31, an executive secretary who came to see me after meeting the "perfect man." The two had known each other less than a month when her new boyfriend "Rod" started pressuring her to let him move in. During our appointment, I shared with Melody my sense that her newfound love would not deliver on any promise he made. She did not heed my advice and moved him into her apartment shortly after they met.

Melody lived in a very comfortable one-bedroom apartment that she could afford on her salary. The "perfect man" wanted a larger unit with a better view. She got the larger apartment and, shortly after they moved in together, other women started to call at all hours of the night. He never did contribute anything for the larger apartment, leaving Melody in dire financial straits. When she approached him about paying his share, Rod threatened her. Melody was the only signer on the lease and therefore, totally responsible for paying the rent she could not afford.

Finally, in desperation, Melody turned to her family to help her in moving out of the apartment. While her credit has taken a big hit, Melody is grateful that she was not hurt. When the "perfect man" could no longer live in her apartment, he found a new victim who allowed him to move in.

All of us are much more powerful than we realize. Regardless of your age, ethnic group or religion, we all want many of the same things. We want to be understood and loved, and the reality is many of us are sabotaging ourselves by ignoring the clues about our relationships that are often right in front of us. The key to our power is that we must live our lives believing that triumph in love is our birthright.

To recap, here are the steps anyone who is dating should take who values their life:

1. Keep your intuition turned on at all times. Allow yourself to notice what you feel about someone before getting intimate.

2. Pay close attention to what the person tells you about his or her past. Whenever possible, determine what facts can be confirmed. Before the relationship turns serious, do a background check on the individual. Take note if they do not introduce you to their family and/or friends.

3. Love yourself and do not make any decisions to let people into your life because you are desperate or lonely.

4. Analyze your relationship mistakes and set the course for making better decisions.

5. Do not walk mindlessly talking or texting on your cell phone. Make it a habit to look people directly in the eye to help you determine if someone around you is potentially harmful.

6. If you feel at risk, take immediate action to protect yourself at all costs.

A well-dressed woman with flawless skin, short blonde hair and blue eyes provided me with one of the most powerful insights into what it takes to overcome a tremendous challenge. Within a few minutes of meeting "Gabrielle," I sensed a deep sadness inside her. My first hint to the underlying stress she was experiencing was the dark circles under her eyes. We were only minutes into our first session when the 50-year-old self-employed designer and divorced mother of two admitted she was often too afraid to sleep.

As part of my intuitive process, I asked Gabrielle to place both her hands on top of mine to allow me to align myself with her energy. The question I ask myself intuitively is the same one that is posed each time a client comes to see me: What do I need to know about this person today? One word came through for me: "offline."

This term is one most of us associate with computers, and it was so unusual I checked in with my intuition again to confirm the answer I received. When I heard the word "offline" repeated again, I decided to ask my client if the word was significant to her.

Looking off to the side for a moment, Gabrielle quickly replied, "I have been saying I am offline since being raped two years ago." Gabrielle looked down at her slim hands in her lap and told me she needed to prepare to testify at the rape trial that would hopefully be scheduled in the coming months.

The forced sexual violation occurred when she was vacationing at an exclusive island resort that she had visited regularly for month-long stays over a five-year period. The major difference in the trip in 2010, when the rape occurred, was that it was the first time Gabrielle had traveled to the island without her husband, as the two had divorced earlier that year. Gabrielle told me she planned the vacation to allow time to heal from the emotional pain of both her marriage ending and the recent death of her father. She invited her 19-year-old daughter, as well as five of her daughter's friends, along for the trip.

From the very beginning, I admired Gabrielle's willingness to be vulnerable and commit to healing this difficult period in her life. She scheduled weekly appointments with me that ended up leading to a few days before the rape trial.

During our first sessions, I noticed that unless my questions were short and direct, Gabrielle would easily get confused. My intuitive sense was that her brain did not process complicated information. We were only a few minutes into our talk one day when I learned that from a very early age, Gabrielle had been diagnosed with a severe form of dyslexia. She had difficultly recognizing words and symbols, and solving math problems. This learning disability presents a number of symptoms across the spectrum.

Gabrielle told me that it was because of her mother's encouragement and dedication to learning that she had overcome most of the staggering problems she faced with her disability.

Sensing that it was easy for her to become overwhelmed, I decided to approach her challenges one at a time. She freely told me about not being able to sleep, and I decided to examine her schedule to find out how we could reduce her stress level. Our first goal was for Gabrielle to go to bed earlier, no later than 11 p.m. Research shows a good night's sleep helps our bodies and minds function more effectively.

Gabrielle also admitted to losing track of time and arriving late to many of her appointments. When she shared her list of things to do with me, it became clear to me that the 25 to 30 tasks she wanted to accomplish each day would be impossible for most people to complete, let alone a person who suffered from a severe learning disability.

Getting her to talk out loud about her challenges helped us to focus on what she needed to do to prepare for the rape trial. At the beginning of each session, we practiced various relaxation exercises, including muscle tensing, deep breathing and EFT, aka Emotional Freedom Technique. A couple of weeks after Gabrielle started to experience restful sleep, we did a short visioning exercise in my office to help her recall details about her attack that she might have forgotten. With her eyes closed, I asked her to tell me about the moments leading up to the rape. After the visioning exercise, she described to me how her rapist lured her to the isolated spot where the attack took place. It became clear to me that it was highly likely from the first time Gabrielle met her rapist five years ago that he was already carefully laying the groundwork to take advantage of her.

Her attacker utilized a technique known as "the trusting game" that crime expert Gavin de Becker describes in his book. Over and over again, for five years, whenever Gabrielle's attacker saw her, he would tell her repeatedly how "trustworthy" he was. I strongly suspect that her rapist recognized the divorced mother's learning difficulties and waited until the time was right to prey on her.

My other top concern in preparing Gabrielle for her day in court was to convince her to break the habit of telling herself she was stupid. It was a common practice for her to start each day going through a list of all the ways she was "not smart enough."

We spent time at the beginning of each of our sessions helping her to visualize how it feels inside when she says positive things about herself. I wanted her to begin each day feeling complete love for herself and focusing on the extraordinary results she wanted to achieve. Gabrielle's homework assignment: Before getting out of bed, she was to visualize her day going 100% the way she wanted.

To complete the process, I assigned her the task of monitoring her self-talk. It did not take long for her to quickly recognize the constant stream of negative statements that she allowed to flow through her mind each day. In addition, I created a list of five personalized affirmations for her to say out loud daily. (An affirmation is a special statement that reinforces positive changes that you want to make in your life.)

It was important to coach her on not being ashamed of her disability. This led to Gabrielle gaining the confidence to tell carefully selected people about the learning challenges she faced.

Another symptom of Gabrielle's disability included short-term memory loss, making it difficult for her to remember a person's name, even when she saw them on a regular basis. As I learned more about her challenges, I had even greater respect for her decision to prosecute her attacker. I am not a doctor and do not profess to knowing everything that is necessary to deal with all types of disabilities, but since Gabrielle sought me out to prepare for the rape trial, each of our sessions involved a great deal of preparation. During the three months we worked together, I read everything current on how the act of rape impacts all levels of a woman's consciousness.

Gabrielle's decision to fight for her attacker to be prosecuted was especially difficult since the rape occurred on an island in the West Indies ruled by the British monarchy. The island's population of slightly over 100,000 also played a part in how Gabrielle came to know her attacker since he owned a local business that her family frequented during the five years they vacationed there. It did not help matters that the island police and medical professionals received little or no training in dealing with rape cases. At the health clinic where Gabrielle went to undergo a vaginal exam, both the doctor and female officer admitted that it was their first time gathering evidence for a rape kit. While lying on the table, Gabrielle told me she felt humiliated when they joked with each other about their "inadequacies" in getting the evidence they needed.

Despite their lack of experience, it was the female officer who played a critical role in Gabrielle's decision to prosecute her rapist. The police officer asked, "If you were to develop HIV from being raped, what would you do to make sure justice was served?"

Gabrielle knew there was only one answer for her. "Prosecute him to the full extent of the law," she replied.

As she shared this with me, I knew intuitively that Gabrielle would start to recall details of her rape, and I advised her to always keep a small notebook to write down any hunches, insights and dreams that came up during the time we worked together.

It is interesting to note that a number of Gabrielle's friends and family members took a very critical stance on her decision to pursue the rape case. After one particularly difficult conversation with a friend who criticized her, she recorded this very poignant dream:

> *"My dog swallowed a bomb. The entire dream is a struggle about what to do. If I tell someone (same thing as sharing anything about yourself), they might take him and blow him up (hurting me too because I love him). If I don't tell someone, then he will eventually blow up jumping off a chair or something and I may blow up with him or someone else I love may be nearby and blow up too. In this case, I will end up hurt for sure by losing him or us both or someone else I love. So do I share myself with others and risk being hurt or do I not keep things to myself and most certainly end up hurt? I questioned during my dream that maybe if I picked the right person to share my problem with, that individual would know how to help me (they know how to safely get the bomb out) and no one gets hurt."*

When I asked Gabrielle her sense of the dream's meaning, this is what she told me:

> "It's a dream about being authentic and vulnerable by sharing yourself with others and the potential pain you might experience by doing so, but also, through the struggle of the dream, the realization that you must take that risk or you will surely experience pain. You can only try to mediate the risk by carefully selecting the people you share yourself with. It was a very bad dream and it woke me up, but I understood it as my dilemma and it gave me great comfort to know that in sharing yourself you will get hurt sometimes but not to worry about it because by not sharing yourself you will most certainly be hurt."

Gabrielle was brought to tears during one family event when she was told that "prosecuting her rapist would only get her island justice, and she would end up a laughing stock." The self-employed designer paid high emotional and financial cost each time she returned to the island to fight for her day in court.

Initially, she hired a local attorney on the island for the case. But the lawyer never returned any of her phone calls after receiving a $10,000 retainer. It was only after hiring legal counsel in the United States that the island's magistrate became more responsive and finally scheduled a date for Gabrielle to give her deposition to the lower court.

Under British law, since her attorney was not licensed to practice on the island, he was locked out from being present during her deposition. The court system did, however, allow the man she accused of raping her to be present as she was questioned.

The court allowed only a lunch break during the 10-hour proceeding.

And during the mealtime, British law was strictly enforced, which prevented Gabrielle from talking to her attorney about the hearing.

After her deposition was taken, it took more than a year before any action was taken by the court to schedule a date for the actual rape trial. During this time, Gabrielle remained focused on believing that one day she would have her day in court and that her rapist would be prosecuted.

During our weekly appointments, I never sensed that Gabrielle hated her rapist. Prior to being attacked, Gabrielle says the warm, caring island people always made her feel safe and protected. Her commitment to them remains so strong to this day that she asked me not to specifically name the island where the attack occurred.

It is all too common for many people to think they are safe from crime when they are visiting a beautiful island resort. While waiting for the trial date to be set, Gabrielle researched various blogs and went into chat rooms of island locals and found there was a constant flow of information on various violent crimes, including other rapes. Of course, the crime numbers on many of the surrounding islands are still much lower than the potential risk we face in the states. The lesson here is very clear: Even if you are vacationing at a luxury resort, you must be alert and keep the same level of concern for your personal protection that you would maintain when visiting major U.S. cities. In other words, keep your intuition turned on.

During the 12-month wait for the rape trial, Gabrielle persistently called her attorneys to follow up with the magistrate on the island. In June 2013, she received official notification of the date for the trial, which was scheduled for the very next week. Many people would not have been able to drop everything immediately and absorb the high cost of last-minute travel arrangements to go to the faraway island. Due to the time restrictions for the trial, Gabrielle had to charter a plane to the small island for one part of the trip. In all, she has spent

$30,000 in legal fees and an immeasurable amount of emotional pain trying to get justice for herself.

While en route to catch the chartered plane to the small island, Gabrielle received a phone call informing her that her assailant agreed to a plea bargain in which he pled guilty to a charge of indecent assault. She was told that he was sentenced to five years in prison and was immediately taken into custody.

Even though Gabrielle was elated to hear this news, something did not sit right with her, and she was intuitively led to continue to monitor websites and blogs to find out if her attacker was actually incarcerated. Little by little, it became clear from various reviews of the island restaurant that the man who supposedly made the plea agreement was not in prison.

Through an inquiry to her attorney, the magistrate informed them that the court felt "the embarrassment of her attacker" was viewed as sufficient punishment. What happened to Gabrielle is all too common: 97% of rapists are never jailed according to the Rape, Abuse & Incest National Network. In lieu of prison time, the court fined her attacker $5,000, which was payable to Gabrielle in one year.

In January 2014, the self-employed designer received confirmation that her attacker has paid the fine to the magistrate.

There is no question that Gabrielle's effort, determination and willingness to fight led to her attacker being held accountable for his actions. She did not care what others thought about her wanting to bring the man who attacked her to justice. Even after she discovered the blatant lie in the court ruling, she followed her intuition and was determined to find out the truth. When we talked during our final session, Gabrielle shrugged off the significance of what she had done to ensure that her attacker was brought to justice. Despite her learning disability, Gabrielle operated at the highest level of mental toughness, a feat few people would be able to sustain.

Today, Gabrielle continues to process all that has happened to her. Despite all the pain and discomfort she experienced, she shared with me the following:

> "I cannot say that I wish it didn't happen because of all of the positive changes, development, realizations, discoveries and maturation that occurred as a result of this one incident. I never thought I would wish for anything but to go back in time and evade it. I can't say that I am glad it happened exactly but I might one day. I do know for sure that he picked the right person to attack in order to stop the damage to the island and the people I love there."

Here are the steps to embrace any challenge as an opportunity for growth:

1. Develop the courage of acting on your intuition regardless if others discredit your feelings or make fun of you.

2. Gain the insight from past experiences and vow not to repeat the same mistakes again.

3. Stay alert and aware to your senses all the time; especially when you are on vacation.

4. Recognize that whenever we go through a violation of any kind, it takes dedicated and committed effort to heal from the ordeal.

5. Be proud of yourself whenever you have dared to stand up to others who have harmed you.

People come to see me for their own reasons. My hope is that when they leave, they are better equipped to face whatever is going on in their lives. This is one of the reasons I like doing intuitive readings; I get to help people with the compelling messages that are revealed. My purpose is to always serve my clients by helping raise their awareness to a problem or an issue that is holding them back.

My work in many ways is like finding the missing pieces of a jigsaw puzzle that helps a person to develop and grow. What I have found is that what stops many of us from achieving our true potential is the deep emotional pain we are often holding in our hearts. Helping a person to become aware of their pain is the reason why I am drawn to doing my work.

Intuition comes in many forms. My process is clairaudient. That is, it allows me to hear a word, phrase or sentence to guide me in my discussion with my client.

A very pretty woman sat across from me in my office one day who looked like she could easily be a model on the cover of a magazine. Even before our hands touched, something told me that she did not live the fairy tale life that her image presented.

As I allowed myself to go into the silence that connects me with my intuitive process, surrounded by a white light for protection, I asked my guides to reveal to me what I needed to know about the person before me that day. Within less than a minute of making my intuitive connection, I heard a word that made my heart skip a beat: "molested."

When the word came back a second time, I felt deeply saddened.

I checked a second and a third time, over and over again. After the third and final check, I continued to hear "molested" repeatedly. When something painful or extremely difficult is exposed during my first intuitive insight, I have learned to allow for small talk to see what unfolds.

What I have found is that what stops many of us from achieving our true potential is the deep emotional pain we are holding in our hearts. Helping a person to heal their pain is the reason why I am drawn to doing my work. The young lady sitting before me was "Linda," 23, an administrative assistant. Her pain was hidden so deeply in her heart that it impacted all of her life choices.

What unfolded in our short time together still amazes me. About 10 minutes into our session, Linda looked down at her small manicured hands and described a love affair like none I'd heard before. A year earlier, she started dating the CEO of a large corporation who had a private plane at his disposal. The whirlwind romance resembled those you only hear about in romantic novels. Regrettably, dating this millionaire playboy caused her pain that surpassed anything I could ever imagine.

Linda's boyfriend had what can only be described as "seasonal relationships." He saw one woman exclusively for each season—winter, spring, summer and fall. During each woman's appointed season, she would be showered with expensive presents and trips to faraway destinations. After a woman's season ended, the high-powered executive would break all contact. Phone calls, texts and emails would not be returned until the woman's "assigned" season rolled back around.

My client had already been through one summer season and knew firsthand the deep pain and loss that came from being dumped before. Despite this knowledge, that did not stop Linda from quickly agreeing to see the millionaire playboy when he called again. She jumped back into the relationship without recognizing the razor sharp pain that was lodged in her heart.

I could feel her pain even before she finished the story. It hurt me to realize that in only a couple of months, this beautiful young woman would be going through the same withdrawal pain that an addict experiences.

After listening to her story, I decided to tell her what came through in my intuitive process. Linda's head jerked slightly when I mentioned the word "molested," and she said nothing for several minutes. It is not unusual for people to need time to process what they have learned during a session. I decided to wait for Linda to break her silence before responding.

After what seemed like an eternity, Linda shared with me another layer to her story which she had only discovered a couple of months earlier. A caring aunt who watched her niece become very depressed and withdrawn when the relationship ended with the millionaire playboy felt it was necessary to reveal a long-held family secret to Linda. The aunt told her niece that a family friend had molested her when she was a toddler. The doctor who treated the little girl told her parents there was no need to tell their daughter about the vile act since "she wouldn't remember it." The parents held firm to this advice and never revealed this painful violation to their daughter. At the time of our meeting, however, her parents were unaware she knew the truth.

As we continued to talk, we discussed the option of her ending the relationship with the millionaire boyfriend before her season ended. I felt that Linda taking back her power was the only way to approach what would soon be another cycle of pain and loss.

We talked about a couple of options to consider, including going back to school to complete her degree and seeing a therapist to help her construct a new life plan. Linda looked right in my eyes and told me that she needed time to absorb all this and would schedule another appointment with me for us to talk the following week.

Linda never returned. That is one of the challenges I have learned to accept in doing intuitive work, that once the person receives the information, they have the free will to decide what to do from that point on. From time to time, Linda still crosses my mind and I always say a prayer for her.

These are the tips to help you access how intuition can play a role in facing the emotional wounds that are blocking your life from being productive and happy:

1. Quiet your mind.

2. Once you enter into a state of peacefulness, ask yourself if you are carrying any emotional pain in your heart? Allowing yourself to be quiet and listen will help you to determine if there's anything that you need to heal.

3. Once you have identified the issue, person or concern that is causing you emotional pain, set the intention to forgive everyone and everything involved. An excellent resource tool that I recommend to my clients is radicalforgiveness.com. The website offers a free worksheet that is password protected, providing an insightful way of healing past resentments, regrets, anger or guilt. The website is the brainchild of author Colin Tipping, who has a book by the same name, *Radical Forgiveness*.

For many people, their children are both their greatest blessing and biggest challenge. Many people could describe their children's defiance, unusual attitudes and behavior patterns as generational. The longer we live, the more we realize how much every generation is different than their parents. This leads us to wonder what causes the generational shift that has many people wondering if children today are more extraordinary than in previous generations.

Many psychiatrists and social workers are calling these extraordinary little people "Indigo children." Indigo children are believed to possess specific, unusual and special traits or abilities. Parapsychologist Nancy Ann Tappe developed this New Age concept in 1982. This field of study involves examining paranormal phenomena, including telepathy, precognition and clairvoyance.

In Tappe's book *Understanding Your Life Through Color*, she describes a rainbow of colors surrounding all live objects. In 1980, the parapsychologist began noticing children were being born with indigo auras. (An aura is a field of subtle energy that surrounds a person's body.) The belief systems of both Hinduism and Buddhism link the color of auras to the seven power centers in the body known as chakras. (Chakras are energy centers in the human body; each corresponds to different glands and governs specific parts of the physical body and areas of the psyche.) These are the ten traits of Indigo children identified by Tappe in her book:

- Come into the world with a feeling of royalty.

- Have a feeling of deserving to be here and are surprised that others do not know it.
- Self-worth is not a big issue.
- Have difficulty with absolute authority.
- Will simply not do certain things (i.e., standing in line is difficult for them).
- Get frustrated with a system that is ritual-oriented and doesn't require creative thought.
- Often see a better way of doing things, both at home and at school, which makes them seem like "system busters."
- Seem anti-social unless they are with their own kind.
- Will not respond to "guilt" discipline.
- Are not shy in letting others know what they need.

There are equal numbers of critics and believers on each side of the aisle who question whether Indigo children really exist. Critics do not believe there's empirical evidence to support their existence. Each of us must make our own decision on what to believe.

It is interesting to note that while in the final stages of writing this book, for the first time, my clients began to seek me out to help with their children. The young people I began to see showed some of the classic signs of being Indigo children.

The first child who came in for an appointment with me was the 10-year-old daughter of a longtime client. "Wendy" looks like a typical pre-teen with long legs and short, curly hair. It was late in the afternoon and the sixth grader seemed a little tired after being in school all day.

Shortly after we first met, I asked Wendy to draw a self-portrait. The sixth grader quickly drew a very large picture that featured her short curly hair transformed into a long, straight hairstyle with two barrettes on each side. We looked at the picture together, and I asked her how her appearance was different from the one she had drawn. Wendy quickly responded, "I look happy, but that is not usually how I feel."

As we continued to talk, I asked the sixth grader to place both of her small hands, palms down, on top of mine as I connected with my intuition to find out the most critical issue she was facing in her life. My inner GPS connected with two concerns that Wendy was going through in her life: being bullied and being in conflict with her sexual identity. As we chatted back and forth, Wendy quickly confirmed that two female classmates had been bullying her. The 10-year-old finally confided in her parents about how she was being threatened at school. Later, both her teacher and the school counselor stepped in and things got better. As we discussed the effects of being bullied, Wendy shared with me a powerful insight: "I won't have very many friends in life. There will only be one or two people, at the most, who will be close to me." Hearing her words that day made me feel like I was talking to a much older person. I decided to wait to talk to Wendy's mother alone to probe the other major issue—a conflict in her sexual identity.

The issue of Wendy's sexual identity was the most important concern to explore since this is often the underlying factor why pre-teens are often bullied, and, in extreme cases, attempt to commit suicide. One of the foremost experts on addressing young people who are struggling with their sexual identity is Dan Savage. In 2010, he created a groundbreaking Internet-based program, It Gets Better Project, for lesbian, gay, bisexual and transgender teenagers as a response to adolescents who have committed suicide after being bullied because they were gay or were suspected of being gay. The project includes over 30,000 video entries from people of all sexual orientations, including many celebrities, and it has reached 40 million views. (You can visit www.itgetsbetter.org to find out more information.)

Talking privately with Wendy's mom that same day was very

important since her daughter already shared with me she "was not usually happy" during our talk about her self-portrait. Her mother, Carol, a 38-year-old attorney, shared with me the astonishing news that from the moment her daughter first began to talk, she told her parents repeatedly that she was gay and that she hoped they would continue to love her. As you can well imagine, hearing those words starting at 2 years old shocked Wendy's parents, and they initially did not know how to respond. They did what most people would do under those circumstances: They changed the subject and tried to distract Wendy with other things.

When their daughter kept bringing up "being gay," both parents tried to figure out where Wendy would have gotten the idea in her head. Her mother told me they did not have gay friends or expose their child to movies or television programs featuring people with lifestyle choices different from their own. As you can imagine, Wendy's mom was deeply concerned about her daughter, especially when she noticed her child become moodier and more withdrawn. The next step we both agreed on was to have Wendy assessed by a mental health professional as soon as possible.

Eventually, the risk of Wendy possibly wanting to end her life became so great that her parents agreed to enroll her in a five-day hospital outpatient program to address teen depression and suicide risk. The program offered a hands-on approach to discussing the stress today's teens are facing.

Teen programs, which offer assistance to high-risk adolescents, will be more commonplace due to the increasing high stress level today's young people are dealing with. According to the 2013 national survey, "Stress in America" from the Washington, D.C.-based American Psychological Association, about 27% of the teens surveyed say they experience "extreme stress" during the school year.

Wendy's involvement in the outpatient program led her to revealing for the first time deep feelings of insecurity that she fought hard to control. It is my belief that both parents initially decided to bring Wendy to see me to explore the issue of their daughter's sexual orientation. Their willingness to deal with this delicate issue, I believe, played a big part in possibly saving their daughter's life. Both parents now fully support their daughter in all facets of her life, including her sexual preference.

Wendy's parents are to be complimented for their willingness to discuss what was going on with their child. It is not unusual for adults to push aside comments made by children who express their wisdom and insight at an early age. Children are highly intuitive and, unlike adults, have not been taught to block their intuition. Many times, little ones will reveal a truth that shakes a mom and dad to their core.

One of the most remarkable accounts of a child's intuitive insight is detailed in the book *To Heaven and Back: A Doctor's Extraordinary Account of Her Death, Heaven, Angels, and Life Again—A True Story*, by Mary C. Neal, M.D. The doctor, an orthopedic surgeon, experienced a near-death experience in a kayaking accident that knocked her out of the boat and left her under water for close to 40 minutes. She was under way too long to survive, and during the time she "died," Mary had a life-changing encounter with God. Her purpose on earth was revealed and she had a newfound understanding of something her son, Willie, told her as a young child.

The author describes how Willie, at the age of 4 or 5, told his mother that he would not live to his 18th birthday. Willie's words to his mom: "You know, I'm never going to be 18. That's the plan, you know it," were like a knife to her heart. She never forgot it and did not dismiss it.

It was during the near-death experience that the angels confirmed the painful revelation that her son would die and that Dr. Neal needed to return to Earth to be the rock to provide support for her family and community after Willie's death.

Dr. Neal categorically states that she believes young children clearly remember where they came from and are still connected to God's world. She says that as children get older, their memories fade.

Willie lived a year longer than his original prediction. His death occurred as a result of being struck by a teenage driver who was talking on a cell phone. In the week following his death, a notebook the family had never seen before appeared on the bookshelf in their home. Willie had written letters to some of his coaches and close friends, thanking them for their friendship. The book even contained a letter that Willie had written to himself. He spoke of the great adventure of his life and how grateful he was for family, his friends, his God and his faith.

It is easy for parents to get so busy and not to notice the warning signs that children often give. Research indicates that by the time children become teenagers, their parents talk to their kids an average of 17 minutes per week.

Clearly, if we want our children to be happy, productive and healthy, we must make time to talk and spend time with them each day. One 38-year-old mother, "Sandy," who brought in her 6-year-old daughter "Juanita" to see me explained how she became aware of how little time she spent talking to her daughter when something was wrong at school.

"My daughter came in from school unable to eat her afternoon snack. When I started to question her about not being hungry, my first grader told me a boy in her class had been threatening to beat her up for the past two weeks." The boy also forced the other kids who sat near her daughter not to play or talk to her. Sandy chided herself over having not been aware of her daughter's distress from the very beginning. After reporting the problem to her daughter's teacher, everyone in the class was urged to speak up if they had a problem with another student.

Clearly, our little ones have access to more information than many of us realize, to help us better understand their needs and also, in some special cases, provide enlightenment to the planet. The critical factor is whether the adults around them will be alert and aware of their own intuition so that they can help guide them in their course. Parents today must teach their little ones to not live solely by the demands of the ego, which is often driven by the desire to win at all costs. And the job of moms and dads who have children who are different is they must not allow their little ones to be shamed or bullied. Children who are encouraged to know themselves are the ones who can develop and grow despite their challenges.

The steps today's parents must take to protect their little ones include:

1. Paying attention to their intuition and discussing anything that does not feel right to them about their child. This includes everything from feelings about medications a doctor has prescribed to talking with teachers and medical professionals.

2. Staying alert and aware when a child tells you that they do not like someone.

3. Setting specific times to have family meals whenever possible and having everyone turn off electronic devices. This will foster uninterrupted conversations.

4. Getting to know their children's friends and friends of their friends. Whenever possible, develop a trusting relationship with the parents and agree to alert each other if they notice anything out of the ordinary with each other's child.

5. Seeking a healer or therapist they can trust who specializes in working with kids who are intuitive.

Suppose you could go to sleep and your dreams would reveal the solution to any problems you are facing? The gift of intuitive dreaming miraculously started for a Chicago businesswoman after a terrible tragedy that occurred when she was a teenager.

The 55-year-old female executive, "Abby," says she will always remember the day when her mother turned up missing after going to work as a registered nurse. She was 17 years old at the time and living in St. Louis with her five siblings when the terrible tragedy occurred. Before that day, the six children, who ranged in age from nine to 20, had grown up with the complete love and support of their mother and father. Her parents had a strong work ethic and each worked two jobs to provide the best for their large family. They owned their own home and spoke openly to their children about the need to be productive. Abby says before her mom's disappearance, she remembers her family as peaceful and loving. This was in stark contrast to the racial turmoil that was going on in St. Louis during the 1970s. She firmly believes that the racial unrest of that period played a pivotal role in the St. Louis police not investigating when her mother first turned up missing. The devastating loss of her mother was compounded even more when her father abandoned the family on the very same day. Later, the six children found out their dad had relocated to California, where he remained for many years.

What makes this story even more puzzling is that Abby's mother prophesized her own disappearance to the three oldest children when they were very young.

"My mother told us," Abby recalls, "one day we would be alone, and that she would go missing and they would find later that she was dead."

Her mother insisted that two things would help her children to survive: Their love of God and the power of forgiveness. Abby's eyes filled with tears when she told me her mother's wisdom became her essence of life as a victorious woman.

Abby shivered slightly as she described the shock of coming home from school and finding out that her mother could not be found. The family was devastated and all the children developed their own coping skills. Five months after her mom went missing, the police found the body, and to this day, her death is listed as an unsolved murder.

A year or two after her mother's death, Abby became aware of the gift of intuitive dreaming manifesting in her life. She believes, without a doubt, that "the gift" was a survival tool to help her deal with this tremendous loss in her life.

Seeking to fill the terrible void in her own life, Abby married as soon as she graduated from high school. The marriage lasted eight years and it laid the solid foundation for a strong family unit that now includes a son and daughter. Abby credits her mom's creative energy as shaping her very core of love and forgiveness.

A smile suddenly crossed Abby's face as she recalled a favorite moment with her mom. The two were walking past an upscale department store when a dress in the window caught her mother's eye. "We rushed in the store and my mom found the dress on the rack and we went into a dressing room where she laid the garment on the floor and examined it from top to bottom. I don't remember her writing anything down. When we arrived home, mom got a piece of black fabric and a piece of chalk and drew the pattern from the original dress from memory. The next morning when I got up, there was an exact replica of the dress hanging on my mother's closet door."

Seeing the dress, Abby recalls screaming and giving her mom the nickname "Magic," which stuck from that point on. She still has a picture of her mother in the black taffeta dress she made that day.

Abby says watching her mother sew is what gave her the insight to know that everyone needs to discover and pursue the areas in their lives in which they feel passion, especially when it comes to being able to find work in today's highly competitive job market. She had this advice for new job hunters, "Young people don't know how to make something from nothing and go out and be able to sell their skill. When you tap into your creative energy, it helps to not only reduce the stress, but your hobby or passion can also provide a way to always support yourself."

This innate ability to create something from nothing is what led to Abby to being handpicked to structure diversity programs for Fortune 500 corporations. Juggling a variety of projects is a common occurrence in the life of this strong-willed power player. Handling difficult tasks is a trademark of her profession, and Abby takes it in stride, saying that her gift of intuitive dreaming makes it possible for her to wake up each morning with the solution to any problem she is facing.

She calls this ability "God's Gift," and she says that it is a natural part of her existence. Recalling her mother's death, Abby feels there is a direct correlation to being anointed with this gift and the tremendous loss in her young life. The gift gave her the strength to face daily darkness and stress. As Abby slept, her strength was renewed, and she felt life was restored each morning.

Being able to create complex solutions to difficult problems in a single night allows Abby to cut through a project in record time. Most mornings start with her grabbing a tablet and quickly starting to write down all the ideas that have surfaced during her sleep. While Abby admits connecting with this gift is a tremendous blessing, she also knows firsthand that it is easy to become overextended and to start feeling anxious when there is so much to do. Her phone rings constantly with calls from people who seek her assistance in a variety of ways.

"Women often end up taking care of everybody else and we don't take care of ourselves. We are the ones who carry the emotional and physical load for others, and it is easy to find yourself strung out to the point where you want to collapse. The solution is very simple: We women must look out for ourselves first. When we do this, then it makes it possible for us to serve others and live long healthy, productive lives," says Abby.

As Abby reflects on the gift of divine intuition she received, she says it brings light, removes darkness and empowers her mind to conquer the impossible.

These are the lessons that occur when we face any perceived hardship, loss or change:

1. Commit to being grateful regardless of any mental, emotional, physical or spiritual challenge you are facing.

2. Recognize the gifts that manifest to help us grow and evolve.

3. Visualize the life you want to create.

4. Embrace your intuition to guide you on the pathway to achieving success and prosperity in your life.

If we look at the world and the challenges we face, many of us are struggling with making the right decisions. If we stay confused, we cut ourselves off from the depth and meaning of what life can offer. When we stop struggling and fully embrace and tap into our hidden asset, our shift focuses from lack to the infinite abundance that is always available to us.

My spiritual teacher and mentor, Connie Newton, tells us to "stay present within our presence at all times." This approach allows us to stay tuned in to every opportunity and learning experience that presents itself in our lives. When you stay present:

1. We realize every experience is a blessing.
2. We take responsibility for all things that occur in our lives.
3. We do not blame ourselves, and others, and instead understand and know that even in what we perceive to be the worst circumstances, we can tap into our hidden asset for clarity and direction.

For many people, it often feels like we are in a knockdown, drag-out fight when we are facing a big decision. The choices you are facing could be anything from whom to love to what bills to pay. The first thing we must do when things feel overwhelming is to remove what is not absolutely necessary for you to do. Our worrying and concerns often block our ability to think intuitively. Do not weigh yourself down with thinking you have to fix everything alone.

What has happened for most of us is that we have simply forgotten to turn to our hidden asset. We need to learn to turn inward for the answers we are seeking. When we do this, we will discover dimensions of ourselves that we had not realized before.

Most of us believe that the world is based purely on our physical surroundings rather than recognizing the power of our inner reality and being aware of how it guides and directs our lives. What blocks many of us from sensing what is going on internally are our own feelings of low self-esteem. The bottom line is when we do not feel good about ourselves, it is hard to trust ourselves to make wise decisions.

Recently, I had a decision to make when an old friend contacted me, "Stephen," who had previously not returned my phone calls for some time. A long time ago, I had to make peace with the fact that, for some reason, he had chosen to no longer be my friend. When Stephen called me a couple of years after my last attempt, the first thing he did was apologize for ignoring my calls and went on to tell me of the very serious surgery he was facing within the next couple of days to repair an aneurysm discovered near his heart. Even though I once experienced hurt feelings when he broke off contact with me, I immediately tried to offer him comfort and support during this difficult time.

Again, Stephen told me that his decision to end our friendship was one of the worst mistakes of his life and he apologized once more. I am glad that I made the decision to be peaceful, making it easy for me to express only love towards him when we talked. Our conversation lasted more than an hour and we both had the opportunity to share heartfelt feelings that we needed to express.

During our talk, Stephen told me he had made other mistakes in his relationships. He had severed ties with his college roommate over a business deal that ended badly. The two were never able to reconcile their differences and unfortunately his former roommate died very suddenly three months earlier. Now facing his own health crisis,

Stephen was openly exploring interconnectedness in life. He asked me, "Do you think my roommate's death is somehow connected to my health crisis?"

"Isn't everything interconnected?" I replied simply.

Very hesitantly, Stephen told me he believed that his surgery would not go well and that he would be reunited with his friend very soon. It did not surprise me to hear that a few days later, Stephen passed away shortly after the surgery. When I reached out to his widow, the shock and disbelief over her husband's passing was very evident in her voice.

"I want to send you a gift," I said right away.

Without specifying an exact amount, I told my friend's wife to expect a check from me. Quickly, I mailed the check while en route to the airport. While traveling, I questioned my hasty action. I asked myself the same question many of us ask when we wonder if we did the right thing. In this silent moment of asking my mind, I retrieved a memory that I had long forgotten.

During my senior year in college, Stephen helped me when I had a near fatal car accident. Being without a car, I desperately needed transportation to drive 30 miles each day to work. Stephen loaned me his prized possession—a spanking brand new Datsun 280Z.

Two weeks after driving it back and forth on a snow-covered, single lane highway each day, a semi-trailer truck crossed the line and slammed into me, causing the vehicle to spin out of control and eventually landing in a cornfield. Even now, more than 30 years later, I can still remember feeling an overwhelming sense of panic when neither of the car doors would open. Not knowing if I was still in the middle of the highway, I realized the only way out was to open the vehicle's sunroof and climb out. If the car had not been equipped with this luxury, I am not sure how long it would have taken emergency personnel to release me from the vehicle. While I emerged from the accident without any physical injuries, my spirit was shattered and it took me well over a year to feel like myself again. Every day in every way, Stephen was there to support me, and even though it took months for his car to be repaired, he never once complained. My insurance provided a loaner for part of the time, but my friend had to continue to make the car note payments all those months that his dream car was out of commission. His passing away gave me the opportunity to revisit the valuable gift he had given to me during an extremely difficult period in my life. The monetary gift I sent his widow was a small token of the love and support I received from my friend. It was because of my willingness to forgive how he treated me that we had the opportunity to talk one final time.

This is what it means to live our lives embracing transformational thinking. Thinking at this level allows the mind and body to heal quickly and to release all feelings of guilt, anger, shame and fear that normally fill our minds and hearts when we are unsure or uncertain if we have made the right decision.

We all have the "right stuff" to connect with our inner being; the doorway to true enlightenment is always open. We must simply make the decision to step through it.

Whenever we are facing a serious decision, the first thing we must do is to consciously force ourselves to slow down. The rapid flow of emails and text messages causes many of us to react quickly without allowing ourselves the time to access our intuition to help us in our process. Research demonstrates that when the mind becomes quiet and brain activity slows, we are able to connect the dots in new ways. No amount of money or technology can replace the inner guidance we have available to use whenever we need it.

The second thing that encourages intuitive thinking is allowing yourself to have time to hear the inner dialogue in your mind. In other words, give yourself time to think and explore without the television, cell phone or any other distraction. Even 15-20 minutes of allowing your mind to freely explore anything that is going on in your life will give you a better perspective of what to do.

One recommendation I make to my clients is to reduce the number of tasks they put on their daily to do list. Keeping your list to a minimum of no more than three or four items allows your mind not to be filled to capacity with tasks that must be completed. Once you accomplish the items on your list, you can always add more, and you will experience a greater feeling of confidence to meet future deadlines.

My third recommendation for thinking more intuitively is to get a good night's sleep. Research has shown that getting adequate rest is highly effective in increasing our mental abilities. Many people cite that they often experience intuitive dreaming to help them solve problems they are facing.

Most of us have become accustomed to multitasking without realizing that the more things we pack into our brains to remember as we switch from task to task, the more our efficiency actually decreases. Handling multiple jobs at the same time weakens our ability to train our brains to put things in the right order of importance, according to Sandra Bond Chapman, Ph.D., author of *Make Your Brain Smarter: Increase Your Brain's Creativity, Energy, and Focus*. Dr. Chapman states that when we keep loading our minds with the constant grind of chores, what results is shallower and less focused thinking.

It all comes down to taking the time to get to know the internal signs in your body. Power is awareness. Our future is based on our willingness to take risks in the present. Decisions become clearer when we are not burdened by feelings of worry or fear.

One of the simplest steps we can take when trying to decide what is best to do is to present both sides of the picture in a pros and cons list. Visualizing both sides of the picture is often enough for us to know what feels right for us to do. At the very least, the list serves as a valuable guide to help you determine what is most important to you in your life.

My client, "Robert," who was facing a major job change, internally, that would involve long periods of time being away from home, compiled his pros and cons list immediately upon being offered a new position. Robert and his ex-wife share joint custody of their two children, both under 12 years old. After reviewing his pros and cons list, Robert made the decision to look for another job rather than disrupt his family. Taking the time to carefully examine his values paved the way for the 45-year-old professional to explore other options for work. And when he revealed to his supervisor why taking on new responsibilities was not compatible with his role as a divorced parent, Robert's employer was so impressed that they gave him a nine-month severance agreement.

The hardest choices we face are often those that involve moral judgment. A recent study shows people make more ethical decisions when their eyes are closed. The reason is that when we block out outside stimuli, we can examine our choices in vivid detail, and this intensifies our emotional reaction. Each us of must make choices that are both moral and ethical. Sometimes the moral decisions we face set the tone for our lives for many years to come. To navigate our lives effectively, we must maintain our own code of ethics. Self-integrity requires that we constantly evaluate ourselves. The challenge is most of us do not know to whom or where to turn when we are facing a decision of this magnitude.

In 2012, Stanford University's Center for Compassion and Altruism Research and Education (CCARE) held the first Science of Compassion conference in Telluride, Colorado. It is amazing to note that research by the founder of CCARE, Dr. James Doty, shows that one in four people living in the United States do not have a single person in their lives to whom they can really talk.

Each of us needs to have someone to share things with, especially when we are facing an uncertain period in our lives. Dr. Doty's research reveals that as human beings, we are wired for compassion, and it is perhaps one of the few practices guaranteed to make us happier.

When we fully engage in helping others, each of us is consciously activating the Law of Reciprocity, meaning that when we do good for others, they are more likely to do good for us. And when we provide assistance to others, this invariably helps our brains grow and expand. This is why whenever you are facing a decision that has you questioning your moral judgment, it is important to create a support team to weigh the matter with you. Try to identify two or three people who have your best interests at heart. For me, the two people who offer drastically different views on things are my husband and one of my girlfriends, and I often go to both of them when facing a challenge that needs careful assessment. Whenever the two of them come with the same solution, I call it "high truth."

Despite having contrasting styles, each of them operates from a space of high moral judgment and I know their perspectives offer keen insight and wisdom to any problem to which they direct their attention. Even by taking all these steps there is no way that we can prevent ourselves from making a mistake.

There is always a chance we can make a mistake whenever we take a risk. The key is not to beat yourself up if things do not turn out the way you planned. None of us is perfect and sometimes what appears to be a mistake is really an opportunity for growth.

It is no secret that all of us make good and bad decisions. That is an occupational hazard of being human. The only way for us to lead full lives is to be open to new experiences and people, which can result in us making mistakes. People who do not make any wrong turns often do not allow themselves to take risks. And when things do not turn out the way we planned, we must release the tendency to beat ourselves up, and instead, view the experience as an opportunity for growth.

Knowing how to shift our emotions is one of the most powerful tools we can tap into during times of disappointment, sorrow and grief. This is the ultimate gift of free will that every soul has available at their disposal any time.

The secret to shifting an emotion is to set the intention to change the feeling that you are experiencing and to replace it with an overwhelming sense of love. Love is the strongest emotion in the universe, and when we choose to consciously embrace it, we are stepping into the role of being a co-creator in our lives. Learning how to do this is the key component to making atonement for our perceived missteps.

Marianne Williamson, in her book, *The Law of Divine Compensation: On Work, Money, and Miracles*, calls atonement a spiritual reset button. "This is a gift from God," she says, "that provides us with the opportunity to clear the karma from past mistakes by owning them, taking responsibility for them, admitting them, making amends for them, and doing whatever is possible to change the patterns of behavior that created the situation that now causes us shame."

Here are six steps for shifting an emotion:

1. Take six slow inhalations and exhalations and allow your mind to become quiet.

2. Set the intention to change the emotion you are experiencing.

3. Visualize in your mind the most beautiful puppy (if you are not a dog person, make it a kitten, or if that does not work for you, make it a baby) and imagine this little life jumping in your arms.

4. Allow the feeling of love to flow through your entire body.

5. Be grateful for the love you are feeling.

6. Repeat, if necessary, until your energy feels renewed and refreshed.

Corporations today are offering more than just lunch to their employees by taking a holistic approach on reducing stress in their organizations. Industry giants such as Google, Aetna, Target, Apple, Nike, General Mills, Goldman Sachs, Procter & Gamble, AOL and The Huffington Post have all created programs to help their workers stay healthy.

These programs include non-conventional classes such as yoga, mindfulness, Tai chi, and ongoing lectures by professionals on health and wellness.

Small companies are following in the footsteps of these corporate giants and are offering their own version of wellness plans. One PR firm I work with brings me in to teach meditation and conduct group visioning sessions to reduce stress and help people be more creative.

At first glance, it may seem that offering these classes is part of the latest "trend" going on in America. The reality is many American businesses are deeply committed to the holistic approach. According to the World Health Organization, they are paying close to $30 billion to ensure the health of their employees.

In 2010, Aetna, the third largest insurance provider in the U.S., joined forces with Duke University School of Medicine to examine the health benefits of yoga. The study found that the regular practice of yoga reduces stress levels and healthcare costs.

Google, the world's largest information provider, offers its employees a three-part course, Search Inside Yourself (SIY), which includes attention training, accessing self-knowledge and building usable mental habits. This innovative program includes mindfulness meditation. (Mindfulness meditation is the ability to be aware of things without the ego passing judgment. Slowing down and choosing to be consciously aware of thoughts and feelings will not make your problems go away, but it can open up your mind to a myriad of ways to handle things.)

These non-conventional programs are the training ground for people to connect with their intuition, imagination and creativity. Research shows that only five to seven minutes of daily meditation can have a dramatic effect on productivity and energy, and also reduces anxiety.

Many of the corporate clients I work with are committed to offering meditation classes to their employees as well as bringing in other health professionals to speak to their workers. More and more companies are replacing traditional brainstorming with group-visioning sessions as a way to create ideas and reduce stress levels.

The goal of a visioning session is to solve specific challenges or problems that an organization faces. The process involves a small group (anywhere from five to 20 people) who perform guided meditation together. When a group meditates and uses its imagination to visualize ideas for solutions the company needs, the process produces a cosmic playground experience where people "play" like they did as small children. A group visioning session is a powerful tool that energizes a team with a deep surge of creative energy. These are the benefits of unleashing a group's imaginative energy:

1. Makes it easier for sensitive issues to be resolved.
2. Allows people to be less afraid to share their ideas.
3. Forms a cohesive bond in the group.
4. Energizes people to take immediate action.
5. Creates ideas that can be easily implemented.

6. Promotes greater trust and respect among the team.

7. Enables more effective collaboration.

8. Serves their customers better.

It is wonderful to experience the powerful reservoir of emotional energy that occurs during a visioning session. The most important thing is to set the intention for everyone to have fun and relax; many people have forgotten how it feels to use their imagination to play like we did when we were children. Using our imagination helps us to gain clarity through self-reflection, which helps to build community and energize a team.

A successful visioning session begins with reviewing the core values of the organization. Identifying the values or core beliefs of an organization is the key to reinforcing the commitment level of your team. When mutually agreed upon values are put into the imaginative field of energy, it is easier for people to become more engaged and energized, and as a result, work more effectively as a group.

One of the hidden benefits of conducting a group visioning session is that it quickly weeds out those individuals who are no longer aligned or committed to the organization's values. This is because the strong energy connections that occur during a group visioning are authentic, making it difficult for people to pretend if they are no longer invested in the company's goals.

This was the case during a visioning session I facilitated for a dance company where 16 people participated in a group meditation to explore new ways to grow their company. At the end of the session, after each person identified their vision for success, the creative director announced to the group it was time for him to leave the job he had held for the last 10 years.

The 40-something male, "Quentin," who stood well over six feet tall, appeared to be visibly shaken when he made this powerful statement:

"There is no separation between my life and the dance company and I cannot live like this anymore."

The group was shocked by the executive's statement because he had been a vital and integral force in the organization from the very beginning. It took almost 20 minutes for everyone to settle down afterwards.

At the end of the session, Quentin pulled me aside to share a photo on his cell phone. The picture he showed me was of a car so mangled that it was impossible to determine the make or model. The creative director was in the car accident two days before our session and walked away without a scratch. Quentin told me that during the meditation exercise I conducted, he completely relaxed and finally admitted to himself that it was time to change his life. Even though the dance company staff did not want to see their creative director leave, they ended the session with openly discussing how they would fill the void his absence presented.

The final portion of a visioning session involves having participants assign teams to plan their activities and set a timeline for completing goals. This is a critical step because a group of enthusiastic people will get more done in less time.

One state government department that participated in a visioning session quickly identified that their phone directory system was outdated and devised a plan for updating needed contact information so that everyone could work more productively. In addition, they decided to reactivate a monthly group luncheon in which all departments would come together and share ideas.

Many people mistakenly think that a large budget is needed to implement change in an organization. In reality, small changes that people "vision" as being most needed are often quickly put into effect and are viewed as being very important to those in attendance.

Large and small companies alike are proving what researchers have told us for some time—that tapping into our creativity, intuition and imagination is a valuable tool for increasing profitability and productivity while also helping employees to stay fit and healthy.

Tips for corporate and organizations to boost the energy in their own visioning sessions:

1. Blast the Pharrell Williams song "Happy" and ask everyone to dance.
2. Schedule your event out of the office in a non-traditional location and make it a "field trip."
3. Ask a broad question that has nothing to do with the company and let the team have fun with it. For example, what are five ways we could reduce crime in the city? How can we stop littering?
4. Give everyone a five-minute limit to draw a picture of the person next to them. Tape the pictures on the wall and see if people can guess who they are.
5. Ask each person to identify what he or she is grateful for.
6. Have a laughing contest and vote on whose laugh cracks up everyone in the room.
7. Toss a beach ball around the room for a couple of minutes.

It is our responsibility to chart our own course for developing our instincts and intuition. We cannot ignore our innate ability to connect with our inner wisdom to help guide and direct our lives. When we consciously commit to using our talents and skills at the highest level, it will become a valuable resource to help us handle any challenges or problems we face.

Our ability to navigate this invisible landscape begins when we are fully comfortable in our own skin. Many of us are distracted from fully developing our intuitive skills because of our preoccupation with outside events and electronics, and are oftentimes blinded by our own doubts, fears and insecurities.

You might be surprised to learn that it actually requires a very short time commitment to develop your inner wisdom. Consistency and discipline are critical, but the benefits will pay off in ways you never imagined.

Periods of quiet and solitude are your greatest ally in beginning this journey. Taking quiet time to reflect on your life journey will often act as a wonderful door opener to you being able to access your intuition. Instead of turning to others for constant conversation and entertainment, allow yourself to become mesmerized by the magnificence of your own soul.

We live in a world that is bombarded with sensory overload. In order to process our inner wisdom, each of us needs consistent and dedicated times of silence so that we can gain clarity and wisdom. What happens to our brain when we experience a constant flow of information is that we do not have the ability to focus clearly. This happens especially when we do two things at once. The more time we spend switching back and forth between various tasks, the less likely we are to be accurate in either task or to be able to access our intuition. In the book *The One Thing: The Surprisingly Simple Truth Behind Extraordinary Results* by Gary Keller and Jay Papasan, the authors cite the latest research that shows that multitasking causes us to lose 28% effectiveness from our workday. This also presents the following challenges in being able to trust our instincts and intuition, causing us to:

1. Develop a distorted sense of the time it takes to complete a task, making it hard to recognize or trust our instincts.
2. Make more mistakes and poor decisions.
3. Experience more stress because we often are not able to "feel" inside what is right or wrong for us.

In other words, switching back and forth between various tasks or jobs makes it impossible for us to know when our intuition is alerting us to the right choices to make. When our brains are so jam-packed with things to do, we waste time waiting for our brain to reorient itself between tasks, making it almost impossible for us to notice when a hunch or awareness slips into our consciousness, alerting us to a possible error.

Often, when my clients first try to access their intuition for a specific issue or question, they will try to force the process and end up blocking it instead. If you are having trouble connecting with your inner wisdom, the following steps should make it easier:

1. Practice meditation without getting frustrated if you cannot quiet your mind.

2. Do not put a time limit on your intuition providing you with a specific answer that you need. Instead, ask to receive the information so clearly that you cannot possibly ignore the message.

3. Be patient. When you begin the practice of paying attention to your senses, you are learning to sharpen your intuition.

4. Ask better questions and focus your awareness on anything that comes in. Many times we look for the big answers, when in reality, our intuition usually presents what we need in small bits of information. Once you become comfortable with recognizing your internal clues, it will be easier to recognize the answer.

5. Express love for everything. We live on a free-will planet and each of us can consciously choose to live in the energy field of love. What we put out into the universe is what we receive in return. When we live in a constant state of love, anytime you notice a subtle shift inside, this will alert you to when something is not right for you.

6. Have confidence in your ability to connect with your instincts and intuition to always guide you in the right direction. Many people ignore their intuition when it tries to guide them on the right thing to do, because of their own self-doubts and fears.

Studies are showing that a regular meditation practice offers improvements in a variety of psychological areas, including stress, anxiety, addiction, depression, eating disorders and cognitive function, among others.

If you do not know how to begin meditating, one of the best investments you can make is to purchase a guided meditation CD. One of my favorites to recommend and use is by Dr. Wayne W. Dyer.

Getting in the Gap, a combo CD and book, offers both a 10-minute and 30-minute meditation that fit easily into whatever personal time you are willing to dedicate.

Even without purchasing a guided meditation CD, you can begin to practice silencing your mind by focusing on nature. The beauty that exists inside of us is one of our greatest gifts. When we silence the inner chaos in our minds, this allows us to fully listen and tune in to our higher consciousness that's there to guide and direct us.

Once you begin and commit to regular meditation practice for at least a month, allow yourself to start to test your intuition in small ways. Start by not looking at the caller ID when your phone rings and allow yourself to "feel" who is on the other end of the phone. When you are traveling in the car, turn off the music and ask to be guided on the best route for you to drive that day. With vigilance, you will notice a sharpening of your reflexes. When we are totally aware of our intuition, it will become easier to deepen the relationship with the most important person in your life...you.

Living an authentic life requires all of us to operate with complete integrity and honesty with ourselves. When we hide our truth because of the need to please others, we are limiting our soul growth and development.

Energy is everything. The best way to stretch our intuitive awareness is by going deep inside and getting rid of fear. This is the greatest gift we all have—the right of free will. We do not have to let outside events rob us of our right to live in a state of joy and peace. No matter how much we are afraid, we can choose to feel love. Each of us can claim an inner core of calm and quiet whenever and wherever we want or need it.

It is not uncommon for people to ask what the intuitive voice sounds like. Consuella Newton gives one of the best descriptions of the higher self as follows:

"It is neither masculine nor feminine and sounds through the vehicle of the mind and conscience. When this occurs for the first time, a person will automatically pause. This cessation of movement causes a feeling of stillness and alertness. There is an accompanying feeling of inner knowing along with alert peacefulness. There is a feeling of 'right action' at that moment."

You will know that your intuition is guiding you because this voice will always have a loving and affirming tone. It does not interfere with our right to free will. This journey inward does not happen without dedicated effort to truly knowing self. Reading books will help, but this will not raise your consciousness. Anyone who wants to connect with their intuition must consistently practice and work hard to sharpen their muscles of inner awareness by meditating.

The responsibility for training your mind to think intuitively means that you must also adhere to "right action." Promises that you make should be kept and your actions should reflect the choices that are in accordance with the highest good for all involved. In the book, *The Four Agreements: A Practical Guide to Personal Freedom* by Don Miguel Ruiz, the author gives what many consider are the time-honored guidelines for what it means to live a life of right action:

1. Be impeccable with your word.

2. Do not take anything personally.

3. Do not make assumptions.

4. Always do your best.

The Four Agreements is an invaluable guide for anyone who wants to live their life embracing a higher consciousness. It is hard for me to keep this book in my personal library, because I often give it to my clients and friends as a first step for taking self-responsibility. Operating in complete integrity requires that we make judgments that reflect the type of life we want to live. We also should require that those who we closely interact with exist in the same level of commitment. Playing on the highest "energetic field" will not keep us free from repeating mistakes. Instead, we know immediately when our actions or thoughts are limiting our own life flow, giving us the opportunity to course correction.

Your journey in becoming aware of your intuition is built on the foundation for connecting with your will and your faith. When we make dedicated efforts to train our brains to recognize our instincts and inner wisdom, this will direct our ability to make better decisions. On a daily basis, each of us must clear the path to connect on all the levels: mental, physical, emotional and spiritual. All of us would like to have a crystal ball to predict what will happen in the future, but the reality is each of us must invest in preparing ourselves for whatever occurs in our lives. Each of us has the powerful ability to discover and become aligned with our hidden asset. Our challenge is to develop this skill and to access our asset whenever it is needed.

Affirmation: A special statement that reinforces the positive changes you want to make in your life.

Amygdala: An almond-shaped matter inside our brain that regulates our emotions. It is very important in our emotional learning.

Aura: A field of subtle, luminous radiating light that surrounds a person like a halo or bubble.

Avatar Program: A nine-day self-empowerment training delivered by a worldwide network of licensed Avatar Masters, guiding others to discovering themselves so they will achieve their goals.

Integrated Awareness: A unique process developed by Consuella C. Newton that links intuition and the conceptual mind for rapid control of awareness in just five days.

Jawoyn: An all-encompassing expression used in reference to language, culture, people and territory of the Aboriginal people who are traditionally connected to south-west Arnhem Land. This area has one of the highest concentrated areas of rock art sites in the world–it's world famous for its rock paintings located in the ancient and hidden site of Gabarnmung Cave.

Mindfulness meditation: The ability to be aware of things without the ego passing judgment. Slowing down and choosing to be consciously aware of thoughts and feelings will not make your problems go away, but it can open up your mind to a myriad of ways to handle things.

Reiki: A healing technique based on the principle that the therapist can channel energy into the patient by means of touch, to activate the natural healing processes of the patient's body and restore physical and emotional well-being.

Shaman: Regarded as a powerful spiritual advisor who can examine the physical, emotional, mental, and spiritual levels of life to aid in the healing process.

Sweat Lodge: A Native American purification ceremony where stones are heated and water is poured over the rocks to create steam. A sweat lodge ceremony is held in a hut that is usually dome-shaped and made with natural materials.

Soma Pi Healing Technique: A preventative and healing health force that is used by certified practitioners all over the country.

Vibrational medicine: A form of alternative medicine that is also called energy medicine and energy healing. It is based on the concept that a practitioner can channel healing into the person who needs care.

ACKNOWLEDGMENTS

Just as my fateful meeting played an instrumental role in helping me on my path, the right people manifested in my life to assist me in setting up a new business model to do my life's work. The persons who played a pivotal role in my decision to use my talents, skills and intuitive abilities are Consuella C. Newton, creator of the Integrated Technique, who taught me everything I know, and Kurt Hill, owner of Holistic Health Practice in Chicago, who welcomed me into his practice and has continued to mentor me in embracing my soul's work. There are also numerous friends who have given me encouragement and support in all areas, especially with the writing of this book. They include my book 'doula,' Marcia Mayne and her excellent team, Rakia Clark, Justin Fulton and Clarence Haynes; Claudene Arrington, Judy Dawson, Ramona Hylton, Liza Antelo, Wanda Lenoir, Rhona Moore, Kevin McGirr, Kevin O'Connor, McGhee Williams-Osse, Judy Teel, Kathleen Scovel, Jewel Ware and Claudia Weddaburne-Bossie, along with a powerful group of women known as the Frilled Neck Lizards who traveled with me to Australia. I will never forget the assistance my cousin, Stephanie Johnson, played in helping me with final editing for my book. All of my siblings—John, Juanita, Horace and Eric Franklin—have given me their love and support as well.

Lastly, I offer my gratitude and deep respect to the wonderful people who have opened their lives and souls to me. It has been my privilege and honor to watch them expand and grow by their willingness to volunteer and be fully present in their lives.

10% Happier: How I Tamed the Voice In My Head, Reduced Stress, Without Losing My Edge, and Found Self-Help That Actually Works — A True Story by Dan Harris

Acts of Faith: Daily Meditations for People of Color by Iyanla Vanzant

An Altar in the World: A Geography of Faith by Barbara Brown Taylor

Anatomy of the Spirit: The Seven Stages of Power and Healing by Caroline Myss, Ph.D.

Ask and It Is Given: Learning to Manifest Your Desires by Esther and Jerry Hicks

The Cosmic Power Within You by Joseph Murphy, D.R.S., Ph.D., D.D., LL.D.

Creating Money: Attracting Abundance by Sanaya Roman and Duane Packer

Discover the Power Within You: A Guide to the Unexplored Depths Within by Eric Butterworth

The Divine Matrix: Bridging Time, Space, Miracles and Belief by Gregg Braden

Do You!: 12 Laws to Access the Power in You to Achieve Happiness and Success by Russell Simmons and Chris Morrow

The Edgar Cayce Remedies by William A. McGarey, M.D.

Giving to Yourself First: Guided Meditations for Self-Acceptance & Self-Esteem by Iyanla Vanzant

Heal Your Body A-Z: The Mental Causes for Physical Illness and the Way to Overcome Them by Louise L. Hay

The Healing Gift: Exploring the Remarkable World of a Medical Intuitive by David Freud with Linda Freud

I See Your Dream Job: A Career Intuitive Shows You How to Discover What You Were Put on Earth to Do by Sue Frederick

The Inner Quest by Consuella C. Newton

Instinct: The Power to Unleash Your Inborn Drive by Bishop T. D. Jakes

The Intention Experiment: Using Your Thoughts to Change Your Life and the World by Lynne McTaggart

Mutant Message Down Under by Marlo Morgan

Out On a Limb by Shirley MacLaine

The Power of Intention by Dr. Wayne W. Dyer

Secrets of Success: The Science and Spirit of Real Prosperity by Sandra Anne Taylor and Sharon A. Klinger

The Spontaneous Healing of Belief: Shattering the Paradigm of False Belief by Gregg Braden

Success Through Stillness: Meditation Made Simple by Russell Simmons and Chris Morrow

Trust Your Gut: How the Power of Intuition Can Grow Your Business by Lynn A. Robinson

What Should I Do With The Rest of My Life?: True Stories of Finding Success, Passion, and New Meaning in the Second Half of Life by Bruce Frankel

Women's Bodies, Women's Wisdom: Creating Physical and Emotional Health and Healing by Christiane Northrup, M.D.

You Are the Answer: Discovering and Fulfilling Your Soul's Purpose by Michael J. Tamura

You Are the Placebo: Making Your Mind Matter by Dr. Joe Dispenza

You Can Heal Your Life by Louise L. Hay

Your Mind Knows More Than You Do: The Subconscious Secret of Success by Sidney L. Friedman

CPSIA information can be obtained
at www.ICGtesting.com
Printed in the USA
FFOW04n1721040216
21166FF